MARITIME ARTS

PLATE I
Herreschoff 12½'s and Doughdishes
racing in Buzzards Bay.
Aquarelle. 12½ x 20. 1980

Notebook sketch.
Arctic whaleman with bomb lance.
Crayon. 1978

PAINTINGS   DRAWINGS   SCRIMSHAW

MARITIME ARTS
BY WM GILKERSON

INTRODUCTION BY JOHN SWAIN CARTER

 COMMENTS BY THE ARTIST

THE PEABODY MUSEUM OF SALEM   MCMLXXXI

PLATE 3
A beachcomber with coconuts.
Pen and ink. 6 x 6½. 1979

Library of Congress Catalogue and Publication
Data:

Gilkerson, William
    Maritime Arts by Wm. Gilkerson
Salem, Mass.: Peabody Museum of Salem
100 pgs.

Catalogue card no.: 80-85092
8101   801201

ISBN: 0-87577-061-4

CONTENTS

WORKS & PLATES

All of the works pictured in this book are of the Peabody Museum of Salem's special exhibition *Maritime Arts by Wm. Gilkerson,* and the catalogue numbers listed below correspond to their plate numbers. When more than one plate is devoted to a single piece, plates subsequent to the first are denoted *a* or *b.*

Of the one hundred individual items catalogued, seventy are illustrated. Of the remainder, some are works in progress as this book goes to the printer, and others were unavailable for reproduction. Some of the scrimshaw pieces have not been pictured; they are illustrated in Wm. Gilkerson's book, *The Scrimshander* (Troubador Press, San Francisco).

Some exhibition items *are* illustrated but not assigned individual catalogue numbers, these being all the vignetted sketches and drawings throughout these pages. They are from one or another of the study-books or logs listed below. Picture dimensions and year of execution are listed by the plates, or, in the case of unillustrated works, in the listings beginning on the next page.

72. *Study book.* CLOTH BOUND, 276 PAGES.

73. *Study book.* LOOSE LEAVES, 48 PAGES.

74. *Log of the* CUTLASS, *cutter, and illustrated journal, 15 August 1961 to 1 August 1962.* CLOTH BOUND MANUSCRIPT, 200 PAGES.

NOTE: The following works are catalogued but not illustrated in this book.

CATALOGUE
NUMBER

75. *Whaling bark* GAY HEAD *and schooner* LETTITIA, *off Cape St. Elias, 13 June 1912.* AQUARELLE: 10 X 13. 1975

76. *Scow schooner* ALMA *in the Sacramento delta with a load of hay bales.* THIS IS THE WORK FOR WHICH ITEM 8 WAS A PRELIMINARY STUDY. OIL ON CANVAS: 22 X 44. 1980

77. BONHOMME RICHARD *sailing on the wind.* PEN AND INK: 8 X 11. 1979

78. *Ships* DUKE *and* DUCHESS, *Woodes Rogers, engaging the Acapulco galleon.* WASH DRAWINGS: 1975

79. *Kosterbot* ELLY *restored to her original rig, c. 1890.* AQUARELLE: 13 X 20½. 1980

80. R/V WESTWARD *off Newfoundland;* A PRELIMINARY STUDY FOR ITEM 35. AQUARELLE: 8¼ X 11½. 1980

81. *Self-Portrait.* AQUARELLE: 5½ X 7½. 1980

82. *Historical view of Marion Harbor.* OIL ON CANVAS: 1980-1981

83. *The artist and Norman Flayderman riding a whale and inscribed:* IF THIS BE GREASY LUCK, TO HELL WITH IT. SCRIMSHAW WHALE TOOTH ON ROSE-WOOD BASE. 1980

84. *Figurehead of an unclothed girl riding a dolphin, inscribed:* MAID OF THE WESTERN SEA. *On the reverse is a clipper ship under studding sails, inscribed:* CALIFORNIA CLIPPER. SCRIMSHAW WHALE TOOTH ON ROSEWOOD AND BRASS SPINDLE STAND. 1977 (SEE The Scrimshander, REVISED EDITION, BACK COVER.)

85. *Walking stick with head of Neptune and dolphins.* SCRIMSHAW. WALRUS IVORY CARVING, WITH SILVER CROWN AND FERULE, ROSEWOOD SHAFT AND STEEL TIP. 1972 (SEE The Scrimshander, PAGES 74 AND 75.)

86. *The whaling bark* CALIFORNIA *being broken up on the Berkeley mud flats,
    1909.* SCRIMSHAW WHALE TOOTH. 1972 (SEE The Scrimshander, PAGE 51.)

87. *A whaling bark outfitting at a San Francisco dock with horse-powered dock
    windlass in action.* SCRIMSHAW WHALE TOOTH ON ROSEWOOD BASE. 1976
    (SEE The Scrimshander, REVISED EDITION, PAGE 41.)

88. *An orca, or killer whale.* SCRIMSHAW KILLER WHALE TOOTH. 1977 (SEE
    The Scrimshander, REVISED EDITION, PAGE VIII.)

89. *White hunter in a canoe on the Congo River, with crocodiles and hippos.*
    SCRIMSHAW HIPPO TUSK ON ROSEWOOD STAND. 1977 (SEE The Scrim-
    shander, REVISED EDITION, PAGES 96, 97.)

90. *Allegorical three-faced head.* CARVED WALRUS IVORY ON A SILVER PLAQUE,
    SHOULDER BAG ORNAMENT. BAG HOLDS A FLEMISH DUDELSAK, WORKING
    REPLICA OF A 15TH-CENTURY BAGPIPE BUILT BY THE ARTIST. INSTRUMENT
    INCLUDED AS PART OF THE DISPLAY. MADE OF BOXWOOD AND WHALE BONE.
    1972 (SEE The Scrimshander, PAGE 77.)

91. *Kerstin with her hair up.* SCRIMSHAW PLAQUE OF ELEPHANT IVORY ON
    COCOBOLO STAND. 1974 (SEE The Scrimshander, PAGE 83.)

92. *Polar bear.* SCRIMSHAW CARVING IN WHALE IVORY, ON ELEPHANT IVORY
    BASE. 1973 (SEE The Scrimshander, PAGES 80, 81.)

93 & (PAIR) *Parody of "old" scrimshaw.* ON THE FIRST TOOTH IS AN HEROIC
94.   HARPOONER, A WHALESHIP AND A WHALE. ON THE SECOND TOOTH ARE TWO
      GODEY'S TYPE LADIES AND A HOUSE WITH DOG. SCRIMSHAW WHALE TEETH
      ON OAK BASE, INLAID WITH WHALE BONE. 1977 (SEE The Scrimshander,
      REVISED EDITION, PAGES II, III.)

NOTE: The following items are all lithographs, remarqued and/or tinted by the hand
of the artist. The descriptions below describe the individual prints displayed in the
exhibition.

95. *Whaling bark* JOHN & WINTHROP. LITHOGRAPH FROM THE ORIGINAL OIL
    (SEE ITEM 42). INSCRIBED: NUMBER EIGHT OF 178, SIGNED AND REMARQUED
    WITH ANOTHER VIEW OF THE BARK, IN PENCIL AND WASH.

96. RANGER *vs.* DRAKE. LITHOGRAPH FROM THE ORIGINAL AQUARELLE (SEE ITEM
    24). INSCRIBED: NUMBER SIX OF 200, SIGNED AND REMARQUED WITH CANNON
    CREW, PENCIL AND WASH. IMAGE: 10¾ X 17.

97.   *Schooner* R/V WESTWARD. LITHOGRAPH FROM THE ORIGINAL OIL (SEE ITEM 35, ALSO THE COVER PICTURE). INSCRIBED: NUMBER THREE OF 750, SIGNED AND REMARQUED WITH SAILORS HAULING ON A LINE, PENCIL AND WASH. IMAGE: 16 X 25½.

98, 99   *Whaling triptych: the three individual panels of the triptych together form a*
& 100.   *single composition which progresses visually and in story from left to right, with the background forms changing from ice to cloud to land, as the three phases of the hunt are shown, with different ships* (CHARLES W. MORGAN, DAISY *and* CALIFORNIA), *from the high latitudes to the tropics, and going from green to blue to purple.* LITHOGRAPHS FROM THE ORIGINAL AQUARELLES. EACH IS SIGNED AND INSCRIBED: NUMBER TWENTY EIGHT OF 128. THE THIRD PRINT IS REMARQUED WITH A PENCIL AND WASH SKETCH OF A WHALE-BOAT AND CREW.

PLATE 2
Men dragging a whaleboat onto a beach.
Pen and ink. 3 x 5½. 1979

INTRODUCTION

I FIRST BECAME FAMILIAR with William Gilkerson's nautical art through a periodical in which some of his water color illustrations were reproduced. I was intrigued by their accuracy, their approach to their subject (which happened to be a San Francisco Bay felucca) and also their handling of perspective. As time passed, I encountered in various other publications more of this artist's work, including water colors, drawings, and oils. Eventually, I found his book *The Scrimshander*[1] and learned that he also created ivory carving and scrimshaw. (The detailing, layout and originality of this has rightly earned Bill the title of the best artist in this medium.) I was much taken with his work and made inquiries about this artist-author-scrimshander. When I learned he lived on the west coast, there ended my quest.

Some time later, while I was visiting with a friend who lives on Buzzards Bay, I was told that a marine artist and scrimshander from California had purchased a gracious old farm down the road in Rochester, and had moved in. Lots of activity was under way there. The place was being fixed up and an old barn was becoming a new studio. Shortly thereafter I spent a thoroughly enjoyable day with the Gilkersons in their new quarters, and saw firsthand some of the artwork which until then I had seen only reproduced (in periodicals and in such anthologies as *In Praise of Sailors*[2] and the National Geographic Society's *The Craftsman in America*[3]).

Bill's work parallels in many ways the work which the Peabody Museum of Salem has collected since its founding in 1799, and his pictures exemplify the kind of art which this institution has traditionally made its special interest—work portraying the maritime heritage underscoring our nation's development. Today we are rewarded for the farsightedness of founders and staff who, over the years, have recognized the value of the work being done in their own times, and encouraged and preserved that work for future times. It is only fitting that we carry on today the tradition as an ongoing program.

William Gilkerson was a natural choice for inclusion in this program in a number of ways. His life has been inextricably tied to the sea since he was 14 years old, when he worked aboard a Norwegian freighter plying between New Orleans and Equador. From that time, he has worked, lived, and cruised on vessels of all types throughout the world. In fact, his present boat threatened to delay the production of this book.

The boat I refer to is ELLY, a Swedish, double-ended gaff-rigged cutter, a Kosterboat, probably built sometime in the 1880's, but perhaps earlier. Having found her and fallen in love with her on a trip to Sweden, Bill couldn't resist buying her when she recently came up for sale. ELLY was delivered to these shores by freighter. By mistake, she was shipped to New Jersey rather than to a Massachusetts port, so Bill had to go to New Jersey, rig his antique, motorless boat, and sail her up the coast to Marion— all this while the preparations for this exhibition languished. Fortunately, he was able to make a speedy return and put ELLY on chocks in time to write the commentary which appears in the following pages. Much of this commentary relates firsthand the experiences which led to some of the compositions.

Experience is a keyword in this work, and it can be argued that the majority of our greatest marine artists, past and present, were intimately familiar with the subjects they chose to paint. It is this familiarity with the ways of a ship that breathes life into the painted surface—familiarity with the routine of shipboard life, the caress of the wind in the sails, or the throb and heat of an engineroom.

Many of William Gilkerson's subjects are historical in nature, but he effectively combines his experiences at sea with extensive historical research to produce accurate and aesthetic depictions. The style of the work is characterized by muted tonalities, limited palette and a stylistic interpretation somewhat reminiscent of ship portraits by some European port painters of the last century, such as the Roux family, Fedi, Toulza and others. It came as no surprise to learn from Bill that he had studied these men, while he sailed and painted in Europe.

Especially, however, this artist is conscious of the human element, and his realistic studies show men interacting around and on their ships and their boats. Men crowd the decks of a Revolutionary War sloop, or a whaleship cutting in a sperm whale. Frequently, these pictures are essays which demonstrate to the close observer the numbers of men aboard the ships, and their individual activities. The symbiotic relationship between man and vessel is easily grasped through such studies.

SHIP PORTRAITURE is one of the two primary traditions in the development of American maritime art. The other is seascape. Sometimes the two have overlapped, sometimes they have gone in their separate directions. It is difficult to say precisely when a distinctly American tradition in marine art began. Certainly the influence of historical European antecedents persists to this day.

Out of an early European influence grew an imaginative and expressive art form with an explicit American orientation. More than most other art forms, maritime painting and especially ship portraiture at its best has examined man's relationship with the natural world that has shaped his life. The storms and calms, the ports and the open oceans, the battles and the peaceful voyages, the fair winds and the foul have all been the subjects of painters past and present in many different schools and traditions.

The Dutch conceived the earliest defined tradition of maritime painting. Their view of ships and seascapes maintained a panoramic scan in which the technological manifestation of the ship rises predominantly in the foreground, or else is seen mid-range. The Dutch brought this perspective with them to the colonies. The horizontal plane of the sea with the tiny shore stations in the background provide the framing or closure devices in the early paintings of these American shores, and the pictures were spyglass views of the New World from seaward.

As the tiny American shore settlements grew and became towns, the men in them who prospered were those connected with the sea, and their portraits survive. Captains and sea merchants from the early times are seen sternly posed with their nautical accouterments about them, their spyglasses, charts and tomes on navigation. Behind them, often through an open window, we glimpse a vessel riding in a placid harbor. The sea is seen as an adjunct to and supporter of American enterprise. A sense of order is present along with a seeking to define the natural world in terms of human control. This is a recurring theme in American marine art through the years and into the present time.

In the nineteenth century, American painting began to develop its own characteristics, combining the conventional panoramic view with an unparalleled optimism that was peculiarly American. Harbor scenes combined ship portraiture with the seascape, and the works of such men as Salmon, Lane, Birch and later Homer and Sloan, all express the artist's individual experiences with the ports in which they lived, and with the vessels that sailed there.

Later, schools of abstraction and the American impressionist tradition attempted more personal definitions, in a manner of speaking, but the realistic approach persisted throughout the twentieth century, and we are currently seeing a resurgence of realism in American marine painting. Indeed, the same seems to be true of American art in general.

Some of today's marine artists are painstakingly reconstructing the ships and events of earlier periods. Through them we are seeing the emergence of the artist and illustrator as legitimate research historian. Other artists are painting the ships and vessels of today, as their predecessors painted those of their own day. William Gilkerson's work spans both categories. It is indeed gratifying to have his pictures in the Museum where they may be viewed alongside the paintings of earlier periods. Through this viewing, we may trace firsthand the thread of development in American maritime painting.

JOHN SWAIN CARTER
CURATOR OF MARITIME HISTORY
PEABODY MUSEUM OF SALEM

[1] *Gilkerson, William,* The Scrimshander, *San Francisco: Troubador Press, 1975; Revised edition, 1978.*
[2] *Warden, Herbert W. III,* In Praise of Sailors, *New York: Harry N. Abrams, Inc., 1978.*
[3] *National Geographic Society,* The Craftsman in America, *Washington, D.C.: National Geographic Society, Special Publications Division, 1975.*

REMARKS ON
SHIP ART

The pictures reproduced here are representative of a particular school of marine art, a school founded in Europe nearly 500 years ago, and which has existed in unbroken succession ever since. This may be called the school of ship portraiture, as distiguished from marine art in general, although there is some overlap. This artist is one of thousands past and present whose work is of this school. In recent years a number of books have treated the broad history of marine painting as a whole, but very little has been heard concerning the particular aesthetics of ship portraiture, or what we shall refer to as ship art. There is just enough space here to permit a fleeting glance at the subject, like a submariner who raises his periscope and has only 15 seconds in which to scan the whole horizon. In our 15 seconds, we shall examine the mystique of boats and ships, and their special magnetism; as well as the elements that make up a ship picture, the qualities required by the picture from its artist, and the place of ship art today, seen from an historical perspective.

SHIP PORTRAITURE may be characterized as a sept of marine art, which is a broad category encompassing many different arts. All of these relate in one way or another to the sea and include graphics, sculpture or carving, and various crafts. The works reproduced here include examples from all three categories, but almost all are graphic, with paintings and drawings in the majority, and some examples of ivory engraving, called scrimshaw. In all mediums, these ship pictures follow the basic precepts of the school to which they belong. That is, they are representational, and they express man and his ships in action relative to the environment in its many moods. All Western artists who work with these common precepts, and who are in some way caught up in the mystique of the ship, may be said to belong to this school. That would particularly obtain to anyone who has been directly or indirectly influenced by the school's originators, the Van de Veldes.

The word *mystique* as used above needs some clarification. It is expressed in a quote from one of the school's greatest exponents in the twentieth century, the painter M. Marin-Marie Durand de St. Front:

I have so often heard old ladies declare that I am "passionately in love with the sea," that in sheer desperation I have had to plead guilty. It is, after all, only a question of vocabulary. . . . True, to talk of "loving the sea" when one means loving the beauty and size of it, or the colour of it, or loving Jules Verne novels or sub-Jules Verne novels, or even loving hot sand and bathing costumes, is, from my point of view, beside the point. It is open to everyone to find what they like in the sea and to love it after their fashion. . . .

For myself, the phrase implies, above all, a taste for boats and sailing; and that does not prevent me from having a more contemplative passion for the sea, which properly belongs to my profession of marine painter.

What is this mortal fascination with ships and boats? How does it happen that generations of artists have been so seduced by their models that they have eloped with them, risking every danger and discomfort? M. Marin-Marie made arduous single-handed voyages across the Atlantic; the Van de Veldes sketched sea battles in pencil and water colour while cannonballs whizzed around their ears, Gordon Grant went before the mast around Cape Horn in a square-rigger, and this list goes on and on. Others have devoted lifetimes to the study of boats and the endless complexities of hull and rig.

Whether these artists have been of the shipboard, dockside or studio variety, they have pursued their subject even during the lean times after marine art passed from fashion, and boat or ship pictures were bought only by patrons as fanatically devoted as the artists themselves to boats—little boats and big ones, old boats, new boats, working boats, yachts, liners, steamers, canal boats, rowboats, square-riggers, canoes, catamarans, freighters, clippers, all kinds, and in their many situations, variously caressed or tossed or spanked by the capricious sea and wind.

Traditionally, boats have been thought of as possessing life of their own, somehow. History and literature are full of ships with their own living personae, evil or benevolent, lucky or unlucky, willful or passive. This may result from sailor superstition or man's tendency to anthropomorphize, to assign human characteristics to animals or inanimate objects; perhaps it reveals man seeing his own life reflected by those things to which he assigns life. However, in a sense a boat does have a kind of life, or at least a living quality which magnetizes man and tugs at him.

The boat would seem to be an *archetype*, a symbol which triggers what may be called the perception of a fundamental reality—the reality of our lives on earth as voyages with definite beginnings and definite endings, and with all the various kinds of conditions in between. The boat, like life, is the vehicle for a voyage.

The boat pulls up its anchors and puts out to sea, committing irrevocably to a common journey (except by death) its captain and common sailors, passengers, cooks, boys, officers and stowaways, along with a few chickens and pigs, maybe a dog, a cat or two, and quite a large number of rats which live in the dark places, emerging in daylight only when the ship itself is in mortal danger. Nor does the company stop there, for there are the worms, beetles, roaches and other tiny creatures which chew, bore, or crawl their way through the whole fabric of the ship. The ship gives passage and nourishment to the lowly as well as the great, and in it, all destinies intertwine. Each being has in common with the others one another's company, invited or not, and (according to his individual endowments) his instincts or muscle, wits and spirits to get him through whatever situations fate tosses his way.

In this way we are all truly in the same boat.

The consciousness of this reality and its underlying implications of adventure are symbolized by a boat, stirring one in its own special way.

There is no wish here to give any offence to people who are more partial to other conveyances such as cars, locomotives, the many kinds of aircraft, horses, and so forth. They, too, certainly have their own symbologies and complexities. It is just that our discussion here is specifically limited to boats and ships and their crews seen through the painter's eye.

In the case of the work in this book, the crews are held to be at least as important as the ships, for although the ships might with their size dominate the compositions, the constant effort has been to portray them as theaters for the human drama.

THUS THE SUBJECT. The effort has been to *express* this subject as truthfully as possible in the three aspects of its existence; its *form*, its character or *spirit* (or feeling) and its spacial framework, or just *space*. Let's define these, for they comprise the anatomy of a ship picture, or of any representational picture, for that matter, and so may be discussed in a context quite a lot larger than just the work in this book.

In this context *form* means the physical forms shown in the picture, that is, ships, men, water, clouds, land, buoys, whatever. The attempt is to render these with a sense of proper proportion and perspective. That is not to say everything must be treated literally, but any exaggeration or manipulation of the form should result from discipline of one kind or another. Again, this is a precept of our school.

In the case of a ship, accuracy of form means making the spars the right length, or the smokestack the right height, the portholes the right size, and all of that. The men should be the right size in relationship to the boat (although some ancient painters glorified the boat by painting its crew as half-sized figures), and the hull should sit in the water correctly. The water and its movement should be in some way understood and expressed. Form correctly expressed is the result of study and good observation of the model.

Ironically, it is difficult to perceive the true form of any large vessel from a near vantage point, because the perspective is distorted and deceptive. A ship is best seen from a distance, where detail is then lost. Further, the observer is limited to the angle of view which accident hands him, unless he is in another vessel or in a helicopter and able to change his vantage point at will.

To many, the ideal situation would be the opportunity to sketch the live vessel in the desired pose, then return to the studio and an accurate scale model of the same ship, plus plans and photos. With luck, the finished composition would then retain some of the flavor and zest of the quick sketches even after being studied, worked over, and edited for accuracy.

4

As to how detailed a ship picture should be, there is of course no prescription for that. How much should be put in or left out is up to the artist. Great accuracy of form alone may make for a very static, lifeless picture, and too much detail may strangle the spirit of the subject.

The spirit is the nonliteral or the off-balance quality of the subject, perceived in a flash. It comes across as a feeling of life rather than a feeling of deadness, or inertness. It is a quality which is not generally found in banknote engravings. The spirit in a ship picture is that aspect which cannot be gleaned from models, books, or plans. Spirit stems from direct observation and experience of the subject and is found more often in the fast sketch than in the carefully contrived composition. Indeed, by its very nature it cannot be contrived. It is accidental, perhaps first appearing even as a mistake. Fortunate is the artist who perceives a happy mistake before he can paint it out. The stroke that captures the spirit of the subject is the stroke that cannot be calculated, for behind it seems to be a consciousness not available in any rational part of the mind.

Form and spirit must be balanced, for even though they describe one another, if they are not in harmony the picture will be either too lifeless or too sloppy. Some artists obviously have tended more to the literal (Cooke, Brooking, Baugean), others to the impressionistic or loose approach (Turner, Homer, Marin-Marie), but whatever the individual's style, he puts form and spirit into some kind of satisfactory ratio.

It is *sometimes* possible to achieve in a picture the spirit of a vessel that one has never seen, if the artist understands from his general knowledge of ships enough to put life into his studies, and to extrapolate from secondary sources the feeling of how that particular hull will ride in the water, and how those particular sails will hang or flap. This usually requires a lot of experience.

Most students find spirit is a more elusive quality than proportion and perspective. Besides the spirit of the boat, there is also the spirit or feeling of the sea, clouds, sky and whatever else is there. Although the artist's final aim is no doubt some kind of unity, each facet of subject will still have its own spirit as well as form.

Lastly, every composition works with *space*, whether consciously or not. It is very ambitious and challenging to work consciously with space, for space is another quality entirely, although it defines the previous two (form and spirit) and is in turn defined by them. Space may be described as that part of the full composition which is not subject or object, although it may be seen to have a focal point of its own, if looked for, as in the spacial vortexes found in compositions by Joseph Maillord, William Turner, and less conspicuously in many of those by Salmon, Willem van de Velde the Younger, and a few others.

Whether expressed explosively, as by Turner, or more suggestively, the space of a composition is the atmosphere which envelopes the picture and unifies it. Conversely, it is also true to say that the forms of the picture must unify with one another in order to express the space in which they swim. It may be hot or cool space, or light or heavy.

Although hard to express with words, space can be expressed visually. Going beyond illustration, the artist describes this space by arranging his forms so that it flows around and through them like water moving through a sunken city, or smoke drifting through foliage. In space-conscious composition, any emotional or narrative quality of the subject is of secondary importance to the dance of form through the molten atmosphere.

WHILE THE qualities discussed above are fundamental challenges to any artist, the ship artist does face some specific problems which are more or less peculiar to his own area of endeavor. For instance, water is a moving mass which solidifies into frozen lumps if painted too literally, and it occupies the lower part of the picture in the most territorial way possible; nor can it be budged from there. How is it unified with the sky, which has entirely different qualities and which occupies the upper part like a warring faction?—And how is that Noah's archetype the boat with its own tactile, textural and architectural presence to be integrated with the other two?

Fortunately, the existence of a potential for actual universality in ship art does not invalidate the many illustrations and less ambitious compositions which comprise the majority of ship pictures. There is obviously great latitude for artistry in the making of an illustration, and no doubt an honest one is many times preferable to a more complex work which is pretentious. Also, in the direct experience of this student, within the illustration is the training ground of the ship artist. Three fundamental tools are learned and practiced, these being what we might term vision, skill with the medium, and exertion.

Having examined the ingredients of a ship picture, let us go a short distance further and glance at the tools with which the ingredients are assembled. They are not complex.

Having a *vision* of something he wants to paint, the artist is inspired to mix his paints—*skill*fully, to the right hues and viscosity—and *exert* himself to paint the whole picture from beginning to end. They interact in any order. For instance, he could *exert* himself to go out and find a *vision* so that he can then *skill*fully paint it.

Exertion is obviously necessary to any endeavor, a picture of a ship or whatever. You exert yourself to get going on it, to keep going on it—through turmoil, tears, obstacles, etc.—and you exert yourself to finish it. It goes like that or it doesn't go. Exertion may be necessary to acquire skill, but does not substitute for it. The sea painter learns skill with the physical materials he uses, oil, watercolor, charcoal, and so forth. He works with his brushes, with his eye-hand coordination, and he learns to be a skilled viewer—both a viewer of his subject and a viewer of his picture through all its phases.

Vision in this sense includes the visual idea which occurs in the eye of the mind at the point of conception. Seemingly, this can be sparked by a subliminal observation, by an idea, or by a conscious observation of something in nature. This may be induced by simply going out and looking around so that the imagination is bypassed. As described by Winslow Homer:

I prefer every time a picture composed and painted outdoors. The thing is done without your knowing it. Very much of the work now done in studios should be done in the open air.

Homer was an Impressionist and was therefore particularly absorbed by the attempt to capture the initial visual impact. Other ship artists have obviously been more architecturally inclined, while still working with impressionism as a tool toward the total picture. M. Marin-Marie was one such. In *Wind Aloft, Wind Alow*, he discusses the subject in relationship to his painter's observation of the sky while sailing the Atlantic in a small cutter:

In the course of this long crossing I saw grey skies, golden skies, skies with clouds like explosions, or cat's whiskers, sometimes one sort tangled up with another (a very bad sign, but that is another point of view), copper skies, skies of an ineffable blue, or of infinite gradations of colour, descending the scale from indigo to livid green, and ranging through golden yellow, cobalt and sea blue, to die away into violet on the horizon.

Understand, it is practically impossible to paint all this: the effect is much too much like a picture postcard! Nevertheless, in the real thing there is no vulgarity. I have seen, on the other hand, harmonies of sweatmeaty mauve which, painted, would make one ill; skies which looked as if they had been painted in sepia; clouds the colour of sulphur, and immense haloes joining one horizon to the other, spreading like a great mantle over me. . . . I have seen seas that refused to harmonize with the skies, confounding the accepted formula, "Water reflects the sky, etc., etc." Yes, I have seen steely seas, cold grey under a most spectacular fantasy of pink and tender blue; olive seas beneath turquoise skies and turquoise seas under grey. . . . I have seen so many apparent improbabilities of the kind, confounding all logic, that one day I ended (the log) by noting at the bottom of a particularly incoherent page, "All, all is possible."

If the picture is to be carried beyond impressionistic study, the vision must include the editing and planning of the composition, and vision plays through all phases of the creation, sparking endless changes and improvisations.

I N 1602 Sir Walter Raleigh complained: *We send into the East Kingdoms yearly one hundred ships, while the shipowners of the Low Countries send thither about three thousand ships.* Logically, both prophet (Breugel) and messiah (Van de Velde) of our Western school of ship art were Flemish and Dutch, respectively. The former, Peter Breugel the Elder, in the mid 1560s made an entire series of ship paintings and engravings in

Antwerp. Most of them depicted warships—galleons and carracks. They comprise the first significant grouping of ship pictures by an individual artist, although Breugel is remembered to art history in general much more for his allegorical paintings and his peasant scenes than his ships. Nevertheless, he was obviouly much smitten with ships, and his pictures of them show great accuracy and reverence. It is conjectured that the pictures were commissions by the owners or officers of the ships, and, if so, Breugel was also the first of the *port painters*, that genre of painters who hung out their shingles in the great ports, painting the shipping and craft on commission. (To a limited extent, this genre still exists, although its golden age coincided with the golden age of sail, prior to cameras, in the 19th century.)

Breugel preceded by more than half a century Willem van de Velde the Elder (1611-1693) and his son, Willem van de Velde the Younger (1633-1707), probably the first full-time, lifelong ship artists and the founders of our school of ship art. Their influence thunders through the successive ages and still reverberates in our own. It is difficult for a ship artist not to be influenced by either Van de Velde, or by some other artist who has not himself been influenced by Van de Velde. That is what makes it a school.

Born in Renaissance Holland, both of the Van de Veldes trained in the time when Dutch painting and Dutch maritime activity were at their zenith. Besides being first-rate artists whose work has seldom been surpassed by any successors, they were without parallel for sheer *gonzo*.

The Van de Veldes were the virtual war correspondents of their time, accompanying the great battle fleets of both Holland and England during the Anglo-Dutch wars, and recording firsthand those elaborate warships in action. This they did either as guests of one admiral or another or from the deck of one of their own yachts. Both were excellent sailors. Their non-combatant status was recognized by both sides, and at various times they had studios in both Holland and in England.

In their hundreds of paintings, grisailles, and drawings, they recorded the shipping of their time in all conceivable poses and situations, for which they received the highest critical acclaim and the patronage of Charles II of England, among others. Largely as a result of their own work and example, both father and son lived to see increasing numbers of artists on both sides of the English Channel working with brush, pen or engraving tool making pictures of vessels.

ONCE BEGUN, the school flourished and spread, reflecting the styles of first the baroque and then the romantic ages. The ship artists of the 17th century recorded the vessels of war, merchantmen, exploration ships, the working boats and hundred of busy harbor scenes, all seen through the dispassionate eye of the age. The 1800s were dominated by heroic themes and the painters who aspired to acceptance in its romantic Academies painted ships as stages for scenes of desperate drama.

The port painters of the nineteenth century continued to center their concerns more around the simple ship portrait. They were an essentially provincial group who made their livings illustrating vessels for masters and owners or for the occasional publication. The work of these men is usually not as ambitious as that of the academics who were their contemporaries, but it is frequently more faithful to the subject.

The port painters were for the most part unaffected by the development of the Academies, which were institutionalized societies formed by an Art Establishment which ultimately dictated its own codified ideas to a beguiled cultural elite. The port painters avoided all this because few sea captains were members of the cultural elite. In point of fact, marine painting, even ship painting, was permitted by the romantic academy, ships being considered appropriate subjects, particularly when involved in some particularly vivid catastrophe such as a battle or a wreck.

Battle and wreckage were themes in the early major canvases of J. M. W. Turner (1775-1851), whose career began during the early part of the romantic movement. He is one of history's most universally admired artists, although, like Breugel, he is remembered more by the non-ship oriented part of the art world as a landscape artist. However, ship art constituted a major part of Turner's work, and whatever else he may have painted, and whatever else he may be termed, he was a ship artist without parallel. His work exemplifies all the best qualities (previously discussed) to which an artist—ship or otherwise—can attain.

Interestingly, he was also one of the first historical illustrators, and he made a number of pictures of vessels which were extinct in his day, just as much as the vessels of Turner's time are extinct in ours. We presume he researched his subject in much the same way as today's historical illustrators, although no doubt with less available material.

Besides being a careful student of ships and boats, Turner conveys a vivid sense of the humanity of the little people aboard them, a strong ingredient of his flavoring. Nor can ships or people be separated compositionally from sky and water, all of which are unified in the heavy, luminous atmosphere which is so thick as to be almost tangible.

Turner himself settled any questions as to his own feelings about his artistic heritage. One day while he was looking at a picture of ships in a storm by Van de Velde, he remarked to some friends who were present:

"This made me a painter."

By that time Turner's reputation had been well established, and somebody protested that his work was far greater than Van de Velde's. Turner is reported to have shaken his head, saying:

"I can't paint like him."

THE 19TH century ended somewhat as it had begun, with studio painters pursuing romantic battle scenes, and port painters busily recording the new vessel types. It is notable that the *List of Merchant Vessels of the United States, 1901,* for the first time contains a more numerous listing of steam vessels and vessels unrigged (barges, dredges, scows, etc.) than sailing vessels, and the vast majority of sailing vessels still working were small coasting schooners. The same was true in Europe.

Sail was on its way out, a situation which had been prophesied in 1839 by Turner in his canvas *The Fighting Temeraire Towed to Her Last Berth.* In it, a veteran old battleship of Nelson's line is towed to the breaker's yard by a little steam tugboat puffing black clouds of smoke against a setting sun. (It should be noted, Turner undoubtedly loved the little tugboat as much as the majestic old sailing ship and loved them together most of all.)

With the beginning of our own century, and as the old ships passed, there came the great revolution which has so much affected ship art. This revolution is generally conceded to have begun with the impressionists' break-away from the stranglehold and endless conventions of the old Academies, letting in some light. Their rebellion was so powerful, it created an entirely new set of conventions which quickly took root and divided the art world in a way the impressionists did not necessarily intend. It was the beginning of the modernist movement in art. In his analytical short history of the Modernists, *The Painted Word*, author Tom Wolfe summarizes it this way:

> *As every art-history student is told, the modern movement began about 1900 with a complete rejection of the* literary *nature of academic art, meaning the sort of realistic art which originated in the Renaissance and which the various national academies still held up as the last word.*

> Literary *became a code word for all that seemed hopelessly retrograde about realistic art. . . . In time,* literary *came to refer to realistic painting in general. The idea was that half the power of a realistic painting comes not from the artist but from the sentiments the viewer hauls along to it, like so much mental baggage.*

In other words, the literary theory of the Modernist school is that viewers standing in the National Gallery looking at Turner's *The Fighting Temeraire* are reflecting much more their own emotions, which have been stirred up by the sentimental scene depicted, than by the painting skill of Turner. Mr. Wolfe continues:

> *What was the opposite of literary painting? Why, l'art pour l'art, form for the sake of form, color for the sake of color. In Europe before 1914, artists invented Modern styles with fanatic energy—Fauvism, Futurism, Cubism, Espressionism, Orphis, Supermatism, Vorticism—but everybody shared the same premise: "henceforth, one doesn't paint* about *anything, my dear aunt," to borrow a line from a famous* Punch *cartoon. One just* paints. *Art should no longer be a mirror held up to man or nature. A painting should compel the viewer to see it for what it is: a certain arrangement of colors and forms on a canvas.*

Wolfe goes on to trace the development of Modern Art through its many phases and into the mid 1970s in his book, *The Painted Word*. This title is taken from the basic concept of the Modernists which holds that the nirvana of aesthetics is achieved only through purging the creative work of anything other than its own self. In the effort to do that, the *isms* have developed, each a discovery of some new item of baggage that could be jettisoned, as though from a wolf-pursued troika. In other words, first comes the *idea*, or *word* of what else can be done away with, then paintings (or whatever) are made to demonstrate this distillation into new realms of purity.

If we seem to have gotten somewhat away from ship art, that is precisely the point. That is what happened. Ship art (along with other kinds) remained pretty much where it was—which is where it always had been since it sprang into being (and pretty much where it still is)—but the word *art* was redefined to disinclude it, along with the schools of landscape, still life, and even portraits, which held out longer, but also eventually fell. Early casualties included all kinds of illustration, anything narrative, and of course anything in any way even slightly commercial.

When the smoke had cleared there was a new regime and there were (as there still are) two arts. There was art, as always, and there was ART. In the previous centuries, the artist had always been just that, an artist, in much the same way a banker was a banker and a politician was a politician, and so on. There was no particularly big deal about it. Under the new order, the Artist was no longer merely artist, but *artist as genius*.

It seems a miracle that ship art has survived the double blow of (a) losing its *chic*, and (b) experiencing the virtually complete extinction of those romantic sailing ships of yore. However, they survived in the canvases of the ship painters who continued to illustrate them.

Perhaps the most noteworthy of these was Montague Dawson, whose illustrations (termed illustrations because of their self-imposed limitation of interest to *subject*) were widely seen throughout the middle years of our century, and thereafter. Why is the name of an illustrator mentioned when this essay has purposely deleted the names of a whole bucketful of artists whose work has been certainly more ambitious, usually more accurate, and sometimes more proficient? Because of all the twentieth century ship painters to date, it is hard to imagine anyone who has had greater influence on the artists of our own day.

Dawson not only survived in the lean years, but he survived rather well, selling his pictures in a market for academic art which continued to exist, even after the Revolution. (This artist first encountered and was immensely inspired by Dawson's work in a calendar hanging in the principal's office in Maryland School in Clayton, Missouri some 32 years ago.)

Dawson was both an historical illustrator and a port painter, depicting many yachts which sailed near his home off the Solent. He introduced several techniques in his ship pictures which have been much studied by his successors. These are readily recognizable and include a kind of carefree handling of the water, which in most Dawsons is splashy and wind-whipped, frequently with transluscent wave tips; his ships fairly leap from the seas, usually under flakey skies, and all are rendered with a combination of control and loose brush work. Part of Dawson's appeal to the modern eye is the unpretentiousness of his pictures. They are of their own time and unabashed in their intentions—or lack of them. He is a self-described student of the paintings of the Van de Veldes.

The late 1970s have seen an increased interest in ship art, and, although the genre is still far from being considered for an exhibition in, shall we say, the Guggenheim Museum of New York, still there is every sign that the school is strengthening itself again.

The question as to whether ship art can eventually free itself from its sentimental image and attachment to heroic themes and bounding clipper ships *a la* Montegue Dawson seems to be already somewhat answered by artists who are painting intricately researched historical scenes, and others who are recording the ships and boats of our own time, the yachts, working craft, commercial vessels and warships, as in the days of the Van de Veldes.

After all's said and done, it is still possible for anybody who can, to make a good picture of a boat. It is this conviction which has inspired the pictures reproduced here, and although they fall pitifully short of the ideals here posed, they are nonetheless an effort in that direction. Such as they are, they are dedicated to Peter Breugel, the Van de Veldes, and J. M. W. Turner, and Salmon and Homer and all the rest, including all of the ship artists today who are carrying on to the best of their individual efforts in the traditions of the school.

W.G.

DRAWINGS & PAINTINGS

PLATE 5
Dean Stephens bending frames.
Aquarelle. 8¾ x 8. 1977

*Workbook sketch.
Pencil and wash. 1980*

West coast shipwright Dean Stephens has built a number of historical craft, although none more colorful than the felucca MATILDA D., *plate 4*, the recreation of a San Francisco fishing boat type built originally by Italian emigrants during the last century. These boats were the original inhabitants of the famed "Fisherman's Wharf."

As a close friend and partner of Dean, and, in 1976 his close neighbor on the Pacific Northwest coast, I had a rare overview of the little boat's creation, from her building in the red barn at the Abalobadiah Ranch boatbuilding school to her purchase by the California State Parks Foundation as a working museum vessel. *Plate 5* shows Dean steaming and bending frames, a picture made from the back of an old pick-up truck.

Besides illustrating the felucca, it fell to my lot to take her out on her sailing trials. This was a particularly adventuresome undertaking. All the felucca sailors were long gone, and nobody could be found who had any real experience with

16

PLATE 6
Felucca MATILDA D. off Aquatic Park,
San Francisco Bay.
Aquarelle. 13 x 9½. 1980

her exotic lateen rig. We had learned that the felucca in its own day was known for being hard to handle and dangerous, even in experienced hands. This reputation turned out to be not unfounded.

Just as I had begun to think I had the feel of her, a gust came whistling in through the Golden Gate and capsized the vessel. A hatch cover was lost, along with an oar, a bottle of rum, and my sketchbook. Boat and crew survived, however, and were ready the next day to sail again, this time for press and public, and with drier results.

Plate 6 shows MATILDA D. approaching Aquatic Park. In the distance is the quarantine anchorage, and beyond that the Berkeley-Oakland hills, with their usual shroud of haze.

Workbook sketch.
Pencil and wash. 1980

17

Plate 7 depicts CUTLASS, previously KALIOPE, an ex-royal yacht. Built in 1896 in Sweden for King Christian IX of Denmark, she was later sold, to pass through many hands and many changes before I bought her (for $1,250.00) in 1961. She was repaired and restored over the course of a long odyssey through northern Europe. Here she is pictured on a wintry Channel crossing between Ostend and Dover. She averaged nine knots that day, triple reefed, with an easterly gale behind her. As we entered British waters, we ran up the Union Jack, and that is the moment depicted.

In *plate 8*, a scow schooner half drifts, half sails with the tide down a slough in the Sacramento delta country. Early morning mist hangs over the water, and the sun has risen just high enough to illuminate the tops of the distant hills. Downstream, a ferry crosses the slough. The scene is c. 1920.

Every summer, hay scows such as the one depicted brought huge deckloads of bales from California's hot central valley down to the Bay Area, via the hundreds of miles of navigable waterways in the Sacramento and San Joaquin deltas. Thus laden, the schooners needed special gear. The tiller ropes were lengthened to permit the wheel's being moved atop a tall platform, where the helmsman stood in order to see ahead. The booms reefed up to the sail (rather than vice-versa) to clear the deck load, which was perhaps six tiers high.

The trip downriver is a windward haul, so tides were heavily relied upon, and, in tacking, the skipper had to be careful to come about before his bowsprit could get tangled amongst the trees and shrubs along the banks. A member of the hard-working family of hay scows still exists and sails on San Francisco Bay: ALMA.

The little sketch of the man sleeping was made aboard a Nantucket ferry. The model was a dozing backpacker. He was shifted 3,500 miles and put atop the hay in the oil painting (item #76) for which this watercolor was a study.

PLATE 7 Yacht CUTLASS off the SOUTH GOODWIN LIGHTSHIP, 27 February 1962; a breezy Channel crossing. *Aquarelle. 12½ x 20¾. 1980*

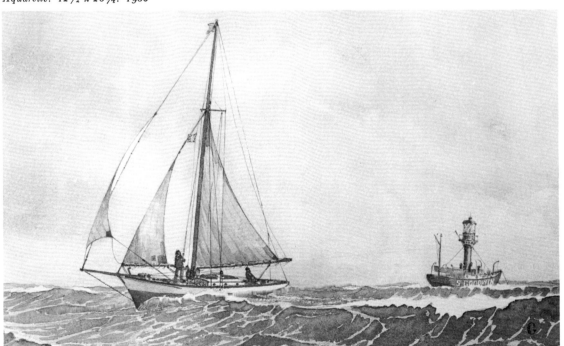

PLATE 8
Scow schooner ALMA in the Sacramento
delta with a load of hay bales.
*Aquarelle study for an oil painting (see item
number 76). 10 x 20. 1980*

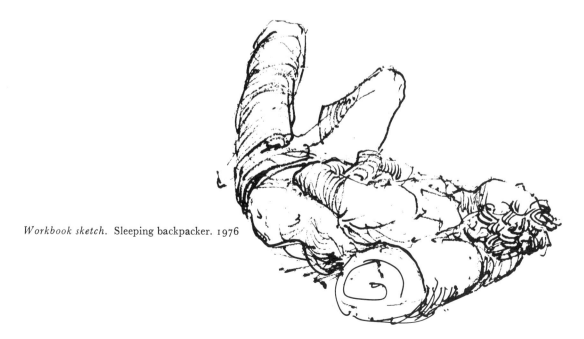

Workbook sketch. Sleeping backpacker. 1976

PLATE 9
Brig SAN CARLOS at anchor off Sausalito,
6 August 1775.
Aquarelle. 12¾ x 9½. 1976

SHIP BENJ. F. PACKARD

Last Voyage, San Francisco to New York ~1924, Sold to Benjamin Flayderman~1929

PLATE 10 Ship BENJ. F. PACKARD on her last voyage— San Francisco to New York; 1929. *Oil on canvas. 22 x 34. 1980*

In 1776 the brig SAN CARLOS by accident found San Francisco Bay, entered it, and on the second day after her arrival anchored off Sausalito. From there, she sent out her launch to explore and chart the surprising area of water into which she had stumbled. This is the scene depicted in *plate 9*. In the distance are Tiburon and Angel Island.

The little brig is one of those enigmatic vessels which played a significant role in history, and was then forgotten by it in all but name. Her type was ubiquitous, the work horse of its day, and so she was not considered notable enough to be marked for remembrance. Research historian Ray Aker combed Spanish colonial records 200 years later and discovered enough about her to enable him to put down her lines, and those enabled the view reconstructed here.

Plate 10 shows BENJ. F. PACKARD. This ship was built in 1885 in Maine, and served in the Cape Horn trade until this century, when she was brought into the Alaska Packers fleet. She was sold again in 1924, when she made her last voyage. This brought her back to the East Coast, via the Panama Canal with a cargo of lumber from the Pacific Northwest. Her owners thought it prudent to have her accompanied by a deep sea tug, in case she needed a tow. As it happened, the tug frequently found it difficult to keep pace with its charge, even though by that date PACKARD's original tall rig had been shortened.

Here, both vessels are depicted: PACKARD getting in her mainsail under heavy skies, with the tug plunging and puffing, straining to keep up. In 1929 PACKARD was auctioned as an antique by Sotheby's in New York.

21

Sir Francis Drake and gun crew aboard
GOLDEN HYNDE.
Wash drawing. 4 x 10½. 1976

GOLDEN HYNDE becalmed off Point Reyes,
June 1579.
Aquarelle. 10¾ x 17. 1976

One of the earliest European visitors to the Pacific Northwest was also one of the most aggressive—Sir Francis Drake, pictured with gun crew in *plate 11*. His GOLDEN HYNDE was a tiny ship of huge historical significance, for she spread terror and hysteria throughout the Spanish colonial empire, striking it in tender areas that had theretofore been thought safe.

We have today only a few thin clues as to how the little ship really looked, but those few make an educated guess possible. The view in *plate 12* follows plans for a model by historian Ray Aker. Depicted is a very weathered little ship, shabby after a long voyage, being rowed and towed in a calm off Point Reyes, California. Drake is thought to have sheltered in the lee of Point Reyes, and even careened there, where there is a favorable beach for that purpose.

Another mood entirely off Point Reyes is reflected in the picture of the small (22′ 10″ o.a.) gaff yawl DANDY, shown in *plate 13* hove to under mizzen only, giving her crew a rest after weathering the point under difficult circumstances. The previous night she had broached on the face of a particularly nasty little sea and put her spreader into the water. *Plate 14* shows her going into the broach.

That particular wave has lived in the memory of our family, all of whom were aboard—including Jackson (then 10 years old) and my wife, Kerstin. It is known as "Kerstin's wave," because she was on the helm at the time it struck. We had been running under only a tiny corner of our roller-furling jib. The log entry which records the experience (preceding the script-text in *plate 13*) reads:

At about midnight we (broached). Just previously I had gone below, turning the helm over

PLATE 13
Yawl DANDY hove-to off Point Reyes,
28 May 1977.
Artist's journal.

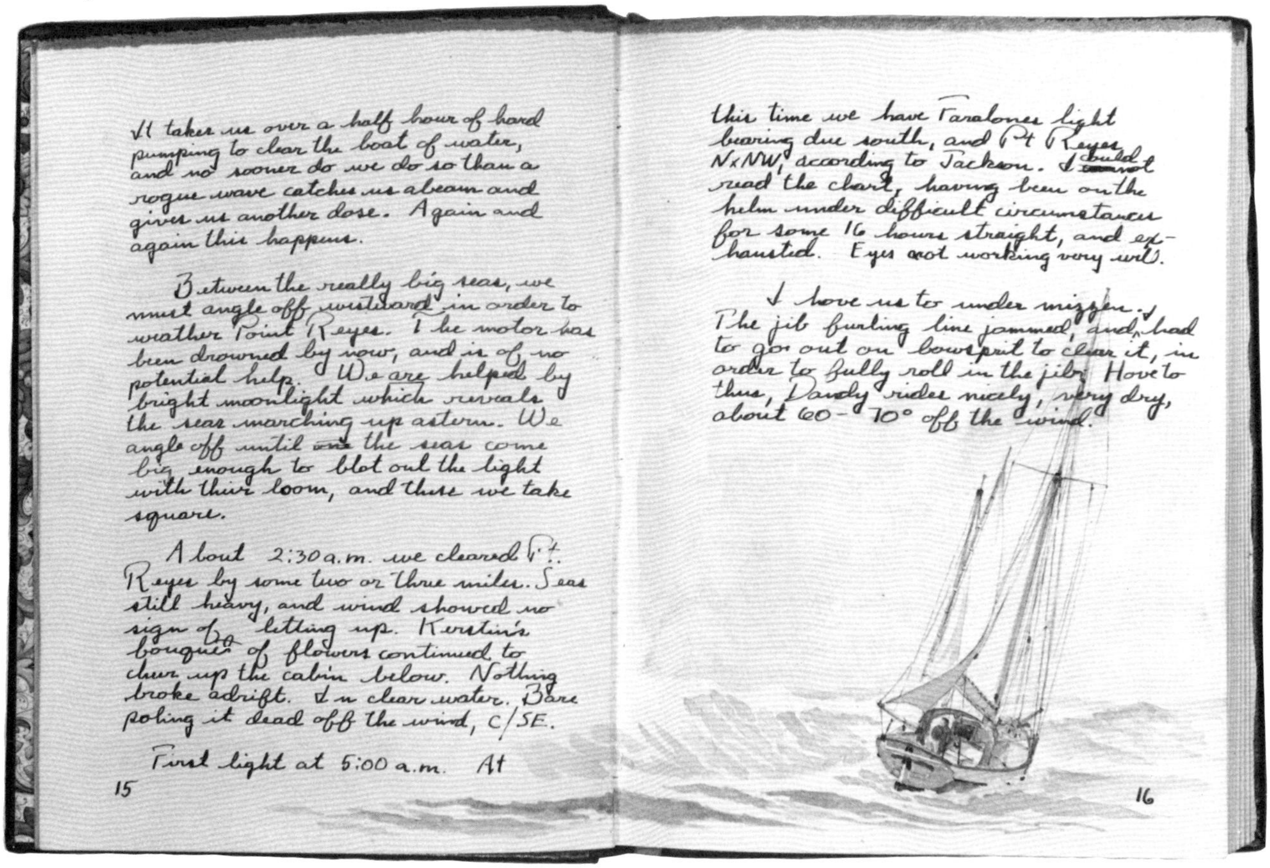

23

to Kerstin. . . . *No sooner got below when there was a crash and a flood of water through the open hatch, accompanied by sounds of dismay from Kerstin.*

Above, I found the cockpit area awash, the limber holes pitifully inadequate drains. Fortunately there was space before the next breaker and time to run off dead before it.

Below, the floorboards floating and a terrified Jackson peering over the top of his leeboard with big eyes. . . . The seas here are huge, and threaten to poop us unless they are taken dead astern.

DANDY is a sister of BLUE MOON, designed by Thomas Gillmer. One of our more memorable cruises in her took us northward along the California coast one January, which is the time of the year when the grey whales are making the same trip, but southbound, from Alaska to Mexico. I was at first concerned about the possibility of bumping a dozing whale at night, which is not as farfetched a possibility as one might think, for most large whales are unalarmed at the approach of a small boat under sail. However, although we saw many whales, they all seemed to be aware of us, and none came closer than 100 or 200 yards. Indeed, they seemed to change course to avoid us.

On a warm, sunny afternoon of gentle breezes, one of our company was on deck having a tune on the bagpipes when a group of whales changed course and came *toward* us, rather than heading away, apparently attracted by the music. They came to within inches of the hull, rolling sideways in the water so they could each cock an eye upward at us. Then they passed under the keel and departed, *plate 15.*

PLATE 14
Yawl DANDY broaching off Point Reyes,
27 May 1977.
Aquarelle. 13 x 17. 1980

24

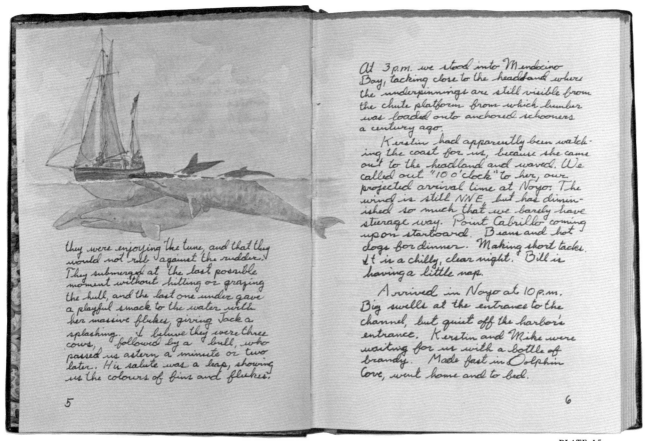

they were enjoying the tune, and that they would not rub against the rudder. They submerged at the last possible moment without hitting or grazing the hull, and the last one under gave a playful smack to the water with her massive flukes, giving Jack a splashing. I believe they were three cows, followed by a bull, who passed us astern a minute or two later. His salute was a leap, showing us the colours of fins and flukes.

5

At 3 p.m. we stood into Mendocino Bay, tacking close to the headland where the underpinnings are still visible from the chute platform from which lumber was loaded onto anchored schooners a century ago.

Kerstin had apparently been watching the coast for us, because she came out to the headland and waved. We called out "10 o'clock" to her, our projected arrival time at Noyo. The wind is still NNE but has diminished so much that we barely have steerage way. Point Cabrillo coming up on starboard. Beans and hot dogs for dinner. Making short tacks. It is a chilly, clear night. Bill is having a little nap.

Arrived in Noyo at 10 p.m. Big swells at the entrance to the channel, but quiet off the harbor's entrance. Kerstin and Mike were waiting for us with a bottle of brandy. Made fast in Dolphin Cove, went home and to bed.

6

PLATE 15
Yawl DANDY visited by Grey Whales,
21 January 1977, off Mendocino.
Artist's journal. 1977

PLATE 16
Ketch GRIFFYN.
Aquarelle. 10½ x 13½. 1980

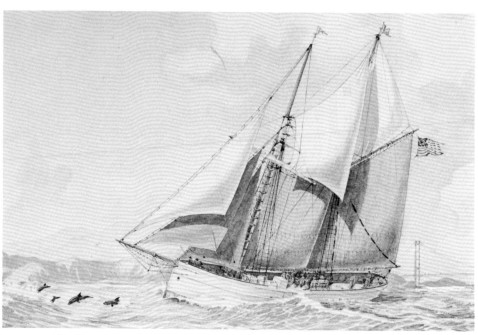

PLATE 17 (detail)
Schooner WANDERBIRD bound out the
Golden Gate, 1940.
Aquarelle. 13 x 19. 1977

PLATE 18
Schooner WANDERBIRD (EX ELBE 2) in the
German Bight, approaching the liner
KAISER WILHELM DER GROSSE.
Aquarelle. 12 x 19. 1977

26

PLATE 19   Schooner WANDERBIRD off Cape Horn, 1936. *Aquarelle. 11½ x 14½. 1977*

Built by H. C. Stulcken of Hamburg in 1884, the motorless lantern-jawed 85′ pilot schooner ELBE 2 served her station for nearly half a century, routinely keeping the sea for long periods in one of the most treacherous areas of the North Sea. In *plate 18* she appears in her professional aspect, under the colors of imperial Germany, approaching the liner KAISER WILHELM DER GROSSE on a drizzly day in the German Bight.

In 1924 she was retired, and some four years thereafter was purchased by Warwick Tompkins, who renamed her WANDERBIRD.

In 1936, Tompkins took the schooner around Cape Horn from east to west, against the winds of the Roaring 40s, an adventure which he subsequently recorded in his book *Fifty South to Fifty South*. WANDERBIRD appears in *plate 19* off the Horn, struggling under triple-reefed foresail and storm jib.

Between 1937 and 1941 she voyaged mostly between San Francisco and Hawaii.

Plate 17 shows her outward bound, the Golden Gate Bridge behind her, and Point Bonita just abeam.

PLATE 20
Sloop PROVIDENCE firing a musket shot at a
British frigate, 1776.
Aquarelle. 15 x 19. 1978

Painting and drawing the various ships commanded by John Paul Jones during the Revolutionary War has been my favorite ongoing professional project over the years. Little is known about these vessels in general, and even less about their construction, rig and appearance. As with some of the other early vessels already discussed, reconstruction is largely a matter of refining the guesswork.

Jones's first command was the sloop PROVIDENCE, and of the handful of clues which exist as to what she looked like, most come from a British intelligence report of February 12, 1776: "PROVIDENCE—a Sloop, all black, low and long with Crane Irons over the Quarters for Oars. 10 guns."

She was reputed to have been a good sailer, and such she must indeed have been, for, in her, Jones made a number of highly successful cruises during which both ship and master proved their capabilities. She seized, destroyed and generally harried enemy shipping along the Eastern seaboard and eluded the many British warships which at one time or another pursued her.

Plate 20 depicts her in a brush with a British frigate. During the incident, the frigate fired futile, long-range broadsides at Jones, who outmaneuvered and outsailed this vastly more powerful antagonist, and in making his escape ordered one of his marines to fire a single, impudent musket shot in reply. That is the moment depicted.

PROVIDENCE would have carried a crew of

PLATE 22   Poster: SMALL SHIPS OF THE SEA. *Lithograph. 26 x 19. 1980*

around 80 or so, of which 50 appear in the drawing in *plate 22*, a poster illustration made for the Museum of Fine Arts, Boston, from a model in their collection. Viewing this picture in retrospect, I find to my chagrin that I have made the sloop somewhat too large in relationship to the men on her, an unintentional discrepancy caused perhaps by trying to get her big *enough*. Many

illustrations done of PROVIDENCE in the past show her too small, and, indeed, I have seen her referred to as ". . . Jones's *little* sloop," or ". . . *little* PROVIDENCE."

Possibly because she had only one mast, she is thought of as a very small craft, but the number of masts is a deceptive indicator of a vessel's size. There is considerable evidence to indicate

29

PROVIDENCE was one of the larger specimens of a type of sloop that by the late 1700s had reached lengths of up to 75′—a lot bigger than many schooners of the day, and as big as some brigs. Indeed, there were full-rigged ships (with three masts, square-rigged on all) of less than 100′. Jones's second command, ALFRED, was such a ship. It is depicted in *plate 23*.

ALFRED was a Philadelphia-built merchant vessel converted by the rebels into a warship. The same British intelligence report that provides our few clues about PROVIDENCE performs the same service for ALFRED, with these crumbs of infor-

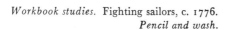

Workbook studies. Fighting sailors, c. 1776.
Pencil and wash.

30

mation: "Alfred—A Ship with a Man head (figurehead), Yellow painted sides Square and Taunt (tall) rigged without quarter Galleries— Guns (32) Men—100."

It should be noted that Alfred was reported to carry only 100 in her crew, only 20 or so more than Providence. This is an aid in conjecturing the relative sizes of the two vessels.

We know from other reports that Alfred was "square sterned." There is some question as to the existence of those quarter galleries. A small sketch reputedly of Alfred shows a vessel *with* quarter galleries. Confronted with conflicting ev-

idence, I have chosen to base my drawing in this detail on the word of the trained observer who witnessed and described the vessels for purposes of identification.

Alfred performed poorly, and Jones desperately petitioned everybody in sight for a better ship. This was eventually given to him.

Ranger was designed specifically as a warship, and was brand-new. She was a ship-rigged sloop of war mounting 18 guns. In her, Jones made a series of raids in the English Channel which brought the war to England. As a result of Ranger's devastating presence in British

PLATE 23
Continental ship of war Alfred.
Aquarelle. 12 x 16. 1978

PLATE 24
Continental ship RANGER vs. DRAKE,
24 April 1778.
Aquarelle. 11 x 17½. 1978

waters, insurance rates went up prohibitively, a large squadron of naval vessels was tied up and militia units throughout the British Isles were mobilized to protect their shores against raids. In the tradition of commerce raiders from Drake to von Luckner, Jones made a nuisance of his little vessel far, far out of proportion to her size.

On 24 April 1778, one of the warships which had been sent to find RANGER did so, and Jones's engagement with HBM DRAKE became the first evenly matched ship-to-ship American victory of the Revolution. The action lasted over an hour. It was described by Jones as "warm, close and obstinate," and it ended with DRAKE's officers dead or wounded, her rigging torn to pieces and her decks "running with blood and rum." (In anticipation of their assumed victory, the British had gotten up a cask of rum which was smashed by a cannonball.)

Plate 24 depicts DRAKE and RANGER in the opening phases of the engagement. Jones can be seen, *plate 24a*, cutlass in hand, a blue-coated figure in the mizzen shrouds. The reconstruction of RANGER was easier than with the rest. Plans of other ships by her designer and builder have survived, and they depict vessels similar in type to RANGER.

PLATE 24a (detail)

The most famous and also perhaps the most enigmatic of Jones's ships is BONHOMME RICHARD, probably the best-known U.S. ship of the Revolutionary War. There exist dozens and dozens of paintings and engravings of her (including many done within months after her battle with SERAPIS) as well as a number of models done more recently. The only consistent thing about these sources is their inaccuracy, however.

Why are even contemporary pictures of RICHARD not accurate? The battle which brought her fame was also the death of her. She sank the next day, after Jones had transferred his flag to the conquered SERAPIS. Many of the artists who hastened to depict the conflict knew even less than we do now as to the actual details of RICHARD's rig and construction. The same was true of SERAPIS. There were no photos, such records as existed were not accessible to the public, and even eyewitnesses (when available) could not help those artists with the technical problems of form and perspective.

The contemporary artists therefore depicted *types* rather than the specific ships. Some artists made no attempt whatever at technical accuracy. As to the models and pictures of more recent times, all those I have seen are wildly imaginative.

The *real* ship has led me a merry little chase for a number of years. Again and again I have stumbled onto bits of data, or new clues as to her appearance, and so have done a number of drawings of her, each more refined in some respect than the one before, and each presumed at the time to be the final statement. This is not a complaint. Indeed, I have grown fonder of the old girl with time and increasing familiarity.

After Jones's successful exploits in RANGER, it was decided to give him a more powerful vessel, possibly even a squadron. Various delays kept him on the beach in France before he was eventually given a 13-year-old French East Indiaman, DUC DE DURAS. This ship (renamed BONHOMME RICHARD after Jones's patron Ben "Poor Richard" Franklin) is variously maligned by historians as having been an old, rotten, slow, unmaneuverable converted merchantman.

Actually, at 13, RICHARD was hardly middle-aged by the standards of the times, and many ships lived to double or triple that age. Whether or not she was rotten is conjectural. Jones completely refitted her, and he would certainly have made any major necessary repairs. As to her speed, Jones did grumble that he could not catch fast privateers in her, but that does not mean she was "slow," merely not as fast as he would have preferred.

Had BONHOMME RICHARD been seriously faulty in that or any other respect, Jones would have howled about it, not grumbled. It must be remembered he had been offered a number of ships prior to RICHARD, and he had rejected them. When RICHARD became available, he accepted her with a certain enthusiasm, writing: "She is

the only ship for sale in France that will serve our purpose."

It should further be remembered that Jones had an eye for beauty, in ships as in other areas. The chances are that RICHARD was a rather graceful vessel by the standards of her time. Most of the contemporary models of French East Indiamen reflect the elegance for which the French shipyards were famous.

The drawing of RICHARD in *plate 25* shows her as she might have looked in convoy with the rest of Jones's squadron on the afternoon before her fateful battle. She is a merchantman of the First Class, with a heavyish bow and the distinctive waterline knuckle peculiar to many French ships of her size. Although a merchantman, she was built to carry a heavy armament, and Jones opened up eight more gunports per side aft on her lower deck, although she carried only six guns there in all.

PLATE 25
BONHOMME RICHARD with Squadron,
approaching Flamborough Head,
25 September 1779.
Pen and ink. 13 x 27. 1977

This and the other pictures of RICHARD reproduced here have made use of recent research by Mr. Norman Rubin, a naval scholar who travelled to France in quest of information about RICHARD and discovered there part of her inventory from Jones's time. Her lines or plans did not turn up, but from plans of many ships of her size, type and age, a composite draft was made. Along with the details revealed by her gear inventory, this draft makes possible as accurate a view of the old ship as we can expect, until something further turns up.

Plate 27 depicts opening guns of the battle between BONHOMME RICHARD and SERAPIS, and represents this artist's best effort to date to depict accurately some aspect of that ferocious and complex night action. The entire battle lasted for hours and was heroically contested on both sides. (Months after the action, upon learning that the British captain who had surrendered had been

knighted for gallantry, Jones remarked: "Next time I'll make him a lord.")

The reconstruction of RICHARD has just been discussed at length. SERAPIS is taken from the draft of one of her sister ships, the frigate ROEBUCK, which is in the archives of the Greenwich Museum in England.

We do not know what sail the ships carried into action, but it is logical to assume SERAPIS was fought under "battle canvas," all plain sail with royal yards sent down. There would have been plenty of time for that during the long approach in light airs preceding the action, and shortening down was the formula in the Royal Navy. It also seems logical to assume that the nervy Jones carried more sail on RICHARD, and that he was willing to accept the risk of its being shot away, and tangling or falling, in exchange for the possible early advantages of speed and maneuverability. These in fact he did gain.

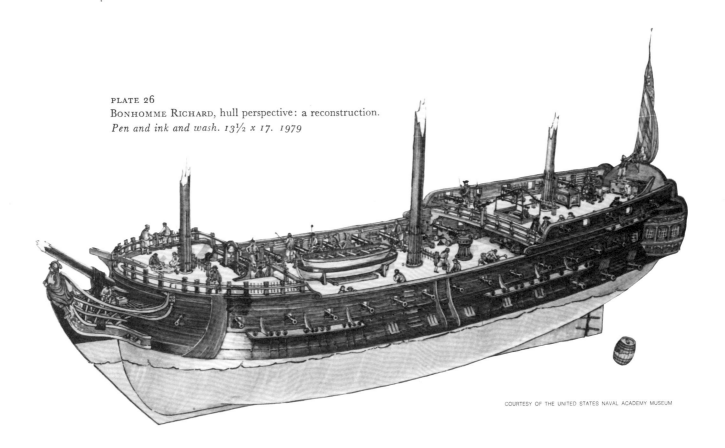

PLATE 26
BONHOMME RICHARD, hull perspective: a reconstruction.
Pen and ink and wash. 13½ x 17. 1979

36

PLATE 27   BONHOMME RICHARD VS. SERAPIS: opening guns, 25 September 1779.   *Aquarelle. 13½ x 23. 1979*

The water was described by eyewitnesses as glassy, but the ships were sailing, which means that air *was* moving high off the water. The picture postulates RICHARD carrying royals and a topmast studdingsail on her fore. We know she was carrying studdingsails only a short time earlier, and there is every likelihood Jones decided to keep it up. It would have been like him to do so. In any case, although SERAPIS turned out to be a better sailer, Jones had his way with her.

The action began at the last twilight, with a nearly full moon described as rising over clouds on the eastern horizon. In the picture, SERAPIS has just rounded to. Both ships have their lower sails brailed up for better visibility. Topmen are seen firing from RICHARD's fighting tops, and this fire was ultimately to drive the British from SE-RAPIS' upper deck. In the background are to be seen other ships that participated in the events of that night.

An expedition has been for some time under way to locate RICHARD's bones on the floor of the North Sea. Should it succeed, we may know at last what BONHOMME RICHARD really looked like.

Workbook sketch. Head of beachcomber.
Pencil and wash. 1979

Workbook sketch.
Schooner SHENANDOAH.
Pencil and wash. 1980

Plate 28 depicts four men along the port side of the main yard of a small bark, furling the mainsail. A bucko mate stands in the top, glowering at the viewer. The picture was done as an illustration for the front and back covers of Volume 5 of *The Mariner's Catalogue.*

On *page 38* are two study book drawings. At the bottom is a 60-second sketch of the topsail schooner SHENANDOAH, made from the flying bridge of a rolling powerboat one summer after-noon in Vineyard Sound. SHENANDOAH was beating in toward Edgartown, and had just begun to get in her topgallant sail. I made several quick sketches with one hand while trying to hold on with the other—not only to steady myself, but to keep my brushes, water and colors from flying away. In these circumstances, any achievement is accidental.

The snaggle-toothed citizen in the wide hat is a Sausalito type who found his way into a series of beachcomber drawings.

PLATE 29
Topsail clipper schooner
PRIDE OF BALTIMORE in four views.
Aquarelle. 13¾ x 33¼. 1979

In *plate 29*, the Baltimore clipper schooner PRIDE OF BALTIMORE sails in a circle so that the viewer may admire her rakish lines from four positions. Although PRIDE is a new vessel, launched in 1977, her builders will assure you that she is *not* a replica. To be sure, her design is of a famous lineage of almost legendary fast privateers which bearded the British during the WAR of 1812, but PRIDE is specifically the work of Annapolis naval architect Thomas Gillmer, for whom this watercolor was made. (Tom Gillmer is also the designer of DANDY; *see pages 23 through 25.*)

During the preparation of this picture, I was invited to join the schooner's crew for a cruise from Mystic Seaport to Halifax, Nova Scotia. It was a fine chance to study an historic vessel in action, and while aboard I had the opportunity to lay out along a square yard, clutching at canvas and feeling for the footropes as the ship foamed along beneath me. It was my first experience of a situation I had many times painted.

Plate 30 reproduces a page from the journal which I kept aboard PRIDE. The drawing shows her firing a salvo from her battery of six-pounders. She did that on every appropriate occasion, to the delight of all. The written text above the drawing is the continuation of a quote from Howard Chapelle's description of the original Baltimore Clippers. It begins:

It would be impossible to write a history of American privateering, the slave trade, or even of piracy, without mention of this type of vessel. The "rakish topsail schooner" is so often mentioned in the voyages of the mariners of the early 19th century, that one's curiosity cannot but be aroused as to the history and appearance of these craft. Generally schooner rigged, they were often engaged in illegal trades—in smuggling in the . . .

40

West Indies and in piracy. Illicit
and desperate practices followed
close in their wakes throughout
their existence.

"The chief characteristics of
these craft were long, light and
extremely raking masts; very
little rigging, low freeboard;
great rake to stem and stern posts,
with a great deal of drag to the keel,
aft. Their deadrise was great and
their bilges slack. The beam was
usually rather great for their length.
Nearly always flush-decked, they
had wide, clear decks, suitable for
working the ships and handling the
guns..."

PLATE 31a   Ancient yawl conceived by the artist:
model by Tom Harsh from lines and plans by Tom Gillmer. 1980

Over the years I have become a confirmed fan of many boats and ships that have sprung from the drawing board of Tom Gillmer, so when I needed a finished design for a little ship of a very unusual sort, I went straight to Tom for its design. The vessel was unusual because it was to be a ship that never was and was never to be, at least in one context. I was (and still am, as this is being written) illustrating and writing a book telling the story of a voyage.

In the course of the story, the boat must be illustrated from every conceivable angle. Obviously, I couldn't use *any* old boat. It had to be just the right boat, and a model was needed so that all the drawings would be consistent. I therefore *invented* the boat I wanted.

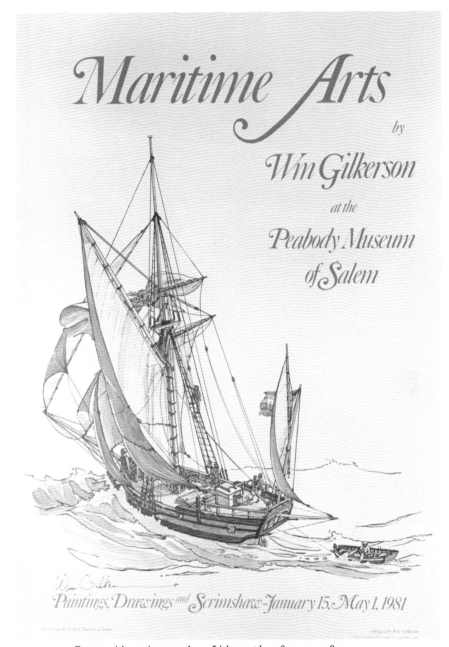

PLATE 33   Poster with ancient yawl.   *Lithograph. 26 x 19. 1980*

It had to be a workable craft, however. I could not give my mariners something which would not properly get them through their adventures in shipshape fashion, so off went my watercolor sketches to Tom. Some weeks later, I received a set of orthographic drawings (identified UFO for Unidentified Floating Object), and, from these, the little vessel was translated into form, *plate 31a*, by the talented modelist Tom Harsh.

To celebrate the launching, as it were, she has been used as the poster illustration for this exhibition, *plate 31*. On it, she is seen driven by a squall which has caught her crew by surprise. They are depicted struggling to shorten sail, bail the launch, and keep matters under control.

Yacht SLY MONGOOSE in the Gulf Stream.
Aquarelle. 12¾ x 20½. 1980

Notebook study. John in action.
Pencil and wash. 1980

Plate 34 depicts a modern ocean racer, SLY MONGOOSE, running from a squall in the Gulf Stream. Portrayed to the left in a 60-second sketch is her owner and skipper.

Until given the opportunity to sail aboard this vessel, my experience had been mostly with older, wooden boats. SLY MONGOOSE was my introduction to a kind of power under sail, which was new to me, and awesome. It also presented me with some elements which I had not previously been called upon to depict graphically.

I was familiar with the wooden pole mast, which in a painting or drawing may be clearly shown bending under strain. But the metal mast, the rigging, and the whole fabric of today's powerful racing machine show no sign of the im-

PLATE 35
Oceanographic training schooner
R/V WESTWARD of the Sea Education
Association, retrieving an otter
trawl off Newfoundland.
Oil on canvas. 26 x 40. 1980

mense tensions which they silently, secretly absorb. Capturing the feeling of this contained energy in a picture is, I think, one of the greatest challenges faced by today's ship artists.

The topsail schooner R/V WESTWARD (depicted in *plate 35*, with the sun shining through her sails) is one of the very few working, square-rigged sailing vessels in commission today. As the oceanographic research ship of the Sea Education Association of Woods Hole, Massachusetts, she spends 290 days of the year at sea, during which time she will log some 20,000 miles. Her function is to introduce undergraduates to various facets of oceanography—and to the ways of a ship.

She makes two study cruises each winter to the Caribbean, and in the summer makes two cruises into the northwest Atlantic, usually to Newfoundland, where she is seen above among ice, with her staysails backed, getting in an otter trawl. In learning about the water environment, her students will examine the contents of the net, finding some cod or haddock, small crabs, sea stars, maybe some spiney urchins.

WESTWARD is a steel vessel of 100′, built in Germany in 1946. In the detail, *plate 35a*, a few of her crew are seen forward, and along the bowsprit, getting in the flying jib. Among the various studies made in preparation for this oil is the watercolor shown in *plate 38*, which established the composition, though it was reversed so that the net could be shown.

45

PLATE 36
M/Y SEA LARK.
Aquarelle. 5¾ x 7¼. 1979

PLATE 37
Herreschoff 12½ PEQUOD
racing in Buzzards Bay.
Aquarelle. 9¾ x 8¼. 1980

Notebook sketch. Walter at the wheel.
Pencil and wash. 1980

I have many times experienced spray coming right over my drawing pad as I've tried to sketch from the decks and cockpits of various small craft. That is all taken in stride. The drawing to the left, however, was whipped clean overboard by the wind and retrieved only moments before sinking by a rescuer in a skiff. By some miracle, the image has survived, although with slightly softer edges than were made by the brush. It depicts the skipper of the schooner FLYING FISH at the helm.

The motor yacht SEA LARK, *plate 36*, is a familiar sight in Marion harbor, as are all the little Herreschoff 12½'s such as PEQUOD, *plate 37*, seen here thrashing past a mark in one of the Thursday ladies' races.

PLATE 35a (detail)
Schooner WESTWARD.
(See page 45.)

PLATE 38
R/V WESTWARD.
Aquarelle study for oil (see plate 35).
12½ x 19. 1980

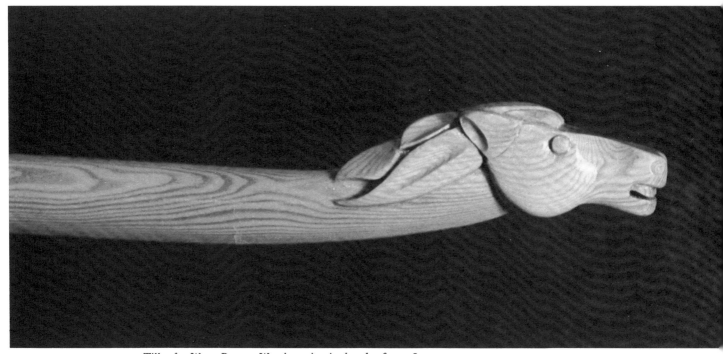

PLATE 39   Tiller for WIND PONY.   *Wood carving in douglas fir. 1980*

PLATE 40
WIND PONY off Bird Island.
Oil on canvas. 9 x 12. 1980

48

PLATE 41
Herreschoff 12½'s racing:
WIND PONY and PEQUOD.
Aquarelle. 9 x 11¾. 1980

Notebook sketch. WIND PONY's skipper.
Pencil and wash. 1980

In this observer's view, the Herreschoff 12½ is one of the happiest small boat designs of all time. The boat in which I have become familiar with the class, and by which I have been thoroughly seduced, is WIND PONY, depicted in *plate 40* passing Bird Island in Buzzards Bay.

WIND PONY was built in 1926 by the Herreschoff yard. Her restoration to "Bristol fashion" has been a project to which everybody in our family has contributed much.

Plate 41 depicts WIND PONY pitted against PEQUOD and others in her class in the hotly contested ladies' regatta. They are here depicted running before a summertime southwesterly breeze, with Kerstin and Kelli keeping up with the pack.

PLATE 42a (detail)

PLATE 42b (detail)

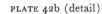

Plate 42 depicts the old whaler JOHN & WINTHROP fishing for bowheads in arctic waters. A whale is alongside, secured by fluke and fin chains. The mates are commencing work with cutting spades, and the skipper stands in the gangway in a green coat directing, while the crew goes about its business. A deckhand coils line into a tub atop the hurricane house, others ready the tryworks, and the cook throws slops over the stern (detail, *plate 42b*). His previous load is seen in the left foreground: an eggshell, a box and a bottle, indicating the bark's angle of drift as she lies hove to, barely with steerage way.

It is not a terribly cold day or the two lookouts in the exposed masthead station (detail, *plate 42a*) would be in the protected box at the topgallant crosstrees, where a man with a waif (a signalling device) is standing by. The empty davits on the port side indicate there are still boats out. JOHN & WINTHROP was a Maine-built bark, registered in New Bedford, and in the last days of the fishery was registered out of San Francisco.

PLATE 42
Whaling bark JOHN & WINTHROP,
out of San Francisco, fishing for
bowheads among arctic ice.
Oil on canvas. 34 x 44. 1975

PLATE 43
Whaling bark GAY HEAD charging the
Webster Street swing bridge,
Oakland Creek, 4 September 1913.
Aquarelle. 10 x 12¾. 1976

PLATE 44
Whaling bark in a breeze.
Aquarelle. 9¼ x 12½. 1980

52

PLATE 45 Whaling schooner LETTITIA and bark GAY HEAD: the last gam, 13 June 1912. *Aquarelle. 10 x 13. 1975*

By the year 1912, there were only three whaling ships fishing out of San Francisco, and June of that year saw the last meeting at sea and gam—a ritual as old as the fishery—between American whaling ships. This is depicted in *plate 45*. The vessels are the schooner LETTITIA (foreground) and the bark GAY HEAD.

The twilight of the whaling industry was not without its tragicomic moments. One such was provided by the skipper of the GAY HEAD, who went mildly crazy after a particularly unsuccessful voyage. In the words of one of his boatsteerers, related years later:

1913 was the year the Old Man came back disgusted. The grounds were just about fished out. He had a good westerly to take him up Oakland Creek, so he blew for the drawbridge, which just got opened up in time, and sailed her right on up onto the mudflats. He would have rammed her right through that bridge if they hadn't opened it.

That scene is conjectured in *plate 43*, which depicts GAY HEAD charging down on the Webster Street Bridge, which was a swing bridge.

Plate 44 shows a whaler of earlier days, under shortened canvas in a breeze.

53

PLATE 46
Whaling bark CANTON
among ice, cutting in.
Aquarelle. 11 x 15. 1975

PLATE 47
Whaling bark OCEAN ROVER.
Aquarelle study for oil (see plate 48).
14½ x 29½. 1979

54

PLATE 48 Whaling bark OCEAN ROVER under the guns of the Confederate raider ALABAMA,
8 September 1862. *Oil on canvas. 22 x 40. 1980*

In *plate 48*, the Mattapoisett whaling bark OCEAN ROVER lies hove-to under the guns of the Confederate raider ALABAMA. In 1862, OCEAN ROVER was homeward bound after a three-and-a-half-year voyage. She was making her return by way of the Azores grounds in hopes of topping off her cargo of oil. As she lay becalmed on the evening of September 8, she was approached by the ALABAMA, boarded, and seized as a prize of war. The whalemen were permitted to make for Flores (some 15 miles distant) in their whaleboats, taking as much gear and as many personal belongings as they could carry.

The weather was flat calm, and they had no difficulty in reaching shore. The following day, two other captured American whalers and OCEAN ROVER were burned.

One of the crew of OCEAN ROVER was Charles B. Hammond, who took with him his sea chest, which is here depicted being loaded into a whaleboat. This painting was commissioned by the current owner of the chest, a Mattapoisett descendant of Hammond.

Although no reference material could be found for OCEAN ROVER, it is known she was built by the same yard that built the whaler SUNBEAM, for which full plans exist. The two ships were built in successive order, and as they were of the same tonnage, this reconstruction is based on SUNBEAM's lines.

Plate 47 is the water color study for the oil. In the final composition, the whaler's position was reversed so the unloading of the chest from the starboard side could be depicted.

Plate 46 depicts the whaler CANTON cutting in among arctic ice, her tryworks smoking.

PLATE 49
Whaling bark CALIFORNIA cutting in.
Pen and ink and wash. 25 x 19. 1980

Plate 49 diagrams the whaling bark CALIFOR-
NIA, hove to and cutting into a sperm whale. All
32 of her complement are shown at their various
activities: another whale is towed in by a six-
man whaleboat; six more men are operating the
log windlass forward; another tails the cutting
tackle line; a hand stokes the tryworks; another
gets a cask into place; under the skids may be
seen the cooper sharpening a cutting spade on
the grinding wheel, turned by the ship's boy; the
helmsman's head is just visible under the hurricane house roof; three more hands wait amid-
ships, along with the skipper, for the cutting to
progress. This is being done by two mates and a
harpooner, from the cutting stage and the chain
plates. A lookout stands at the fore crosstrees
with a waif, ready to signal the boat still out,
plate 50; his relief makes his way aloft. The whale
alongside is of medium size, about 40 feet in
length. The one under tow is smaller. Both are
being attacked by the usual swarm of blue sharks.

PLATE 50
A boat from the CALIFORNIA pursuing whales.
A companion piece to item 49.
Pen and ink and wash. 9 x 7. 1980

PLATE 49a (detail)

PLATE 51
QUEQUEG and ISHMAEL
accosted by ELIJA.
*Scrimshaw whale tooth on
rosewood base. 1978*

58

SCRIMSHAW

ART NEVER comes off worse than when undergoing *definition* at the hands of scholars, writers or theorists. The shipboard art of ivory engraving called scrimshaw has suffered more than most from the definition disease, beginning with the name *scrimshaw* itself. Nobody seems to know where the word came from, or what it originally meant, if anything, although conflicting theories abound.

Besides not knowing the meaning of the word, scholars have a surprising amount of trouble getting together on what can and what cannot be defined as *being* scrimshaw. Some hold it to be exclusively work done on ships, whereas others contend it isn't scrimshaw if it wasn't done on a *whaling* ship, and still others feel that any *maritime*-inspired work of the ilk is still scrimshaw, although there is a controversy as to the validity of old vs. new scrimshaw, with its question as to whether new scrimshaw is scrimshaw at all.

Some have it scrimshaw died with the *whaling* industry, and others say it is America's only indigenous, non-aboriginal art. Others still define it

as a *craft*. Most authorities agree it is a *folk art*. Some insist it be more narrowly defined as a *marine* folk art. It has been referred to by one source as a *primary* folk art, by another as a *secondary art* (eschewing "folk") and the least generous of all has branded it *not* an art. What is ever a poor soul to believe? For academic purposes the following consolidation is proposed:

Scrimshaw: A primary marine folk craft with secondary characteristics; also the non-art of American Whalemen and others perhaps dead.

Let us pass the point.

The first scrimshaw seems to have been done around the mid-1600s aboard Dutch arctic whaleships, work consisting of small crafted or carved artifacts made from bone or baleen. When the American whalemen came along, they also did this type of work and because they fished for sperm whales, which have ivory teeth, they were able to introduce the engraved whale's tooth into the scrimshaw repertory, probably around 1800 or so.

Generally speaking, a tooth is scrimshaw'd something like this: it is first polished down by sanding or scraping, and then a design is scratched, gouged, stippled or cut into the surface of the ivory with a scribe, engraving tool, stipple-point or knife. The wounds are pigmented with ink or paint, and then the surface is repolished so that the design remains. All of the pieces of scrimshaw here reproduced are of this variety.

Scrimshaw was common work on many ships throughout the last century and into this one. After the death of the American sailing whaling industry, it was still carried on by a few men ashore. Some of them were retired whalemen. Others did it simply because the medium appealed to

them, and whale teeth were easily obtained. There remained a small tourist market for such new work, despite the large quantities of old scrimshaw which were to be found in all the places where whaling ships had regularly touched.

For the most part, the original teeth were unskillfully done, unsigned and therefore uninteresting to all but a few enthusiasts. In its own day, the art never had a chronicler, and next to nothing is known of the individuals who made it. Partly for these reasons, there is no lineage of scrimshaw artists as with ship painters, although the art originated in Dutch ships at the time of Van de Velde. The early scrimshanders were men unschooled in the pursuit, therefore they may definitively be called primitive artists. The charm of the early work, where charm exists, is usually embodied in the primitive quality of the work, rather than in the facility of its execution.

IN THE early 1960s there was a kind of rediscovery of scrimshaw, probably sparked by President John F. Kennedy, who was a conspicuous scrimshaw collector. As a result, antique scrimshaw was bought up by collectors and new scrimshaw appeared everywhere.

Much of the new scrimshaw consisted of trinketry done on a production-line basis (tie tacks, cuff links, desk sets). Whale teeth were engraved, generally imitating as closely as possible the primitive styles of the old work. Many forgeries of old work inevitably appeared. The materials—whale's teeth—for this mini-industry were supplied primarily by the Japanese, who maintained an active sperm whale fishery and exported many tons of whale ivory into the United States.

This artist's first scrimshaw'd whale tooth was produced around 1968 in San Francisco, a picture of the ketch GRIFFYN. It was made with no

PLATE 52
Steam barkentines, plus a sailing bark and a distant schooner.
Scrimshaw triptych on elephant ivory
plaques; lignum vitae base. 1979

PLATE 53 A dock scene with a whaler fitting out. *Scrimshaw. Whale tooth on rosewood base. 1979*

attempt at imitating any kind of primitive style. Indeed, the artist was largely unaware of what the old style was, never having particularly studied it.

The attempt was (then as now) to make a picture on the tooth's surface which was compatible with the whole form of the object, as opposed to trying to make the picture flat. It was great fun, and led to the purchase of a lot of Japanese whale teeth from a Sausalito gift shop, all of which were avidly scratched, then given away to various friends.

THE COMPLAINT heard most frequently in connection with today's scrimshaw is that so much of it is junk. No doubt this is all too true, but it must be borne in mind that there is generally a lot more forgettable work done than memorable work, with the result that the former is indeed forgotten in time, while the memorable work survives. Great mountains of junk art of all kinds have been created and then absorbed by time. The trinket scrimshaw of today seems so overwhelmingly profuse because it has not yet had enough time in which to vanish.

Second, even the best of artists have to make their bad work in order to learn what the good is. One very good thing about the trinket scrimshaw industry is that a few of the people who worked in it have used it as a good opportunity to practice the art and develop it beyond production of imitative trivia—sometimes to a point of excellence. By this process, scrimshaw has metamorphosed. It is no longer a primitive art. It may still be a marine art (as here), but even that distinction has fallen away in the case of some who do no nautical work at all. Does that mean it is no longer scrimshaw? Let us throw that back to the art theorists and move along.

ALTHOUGH scrimshaw has had no line of teachers to pass along one to another the techniques and methods of the art, the same criteria obtain to scrimshaw as to painting or drawing: form and spirit of the subject depicted in a spacially correct composition. The limiting factors to scrimshaw are having to work with line only, and having to work within the accidental form of the whale's tooth—if whale's-tooth scrimshaw it is.

As to the limitation of line, that is also the limitation in copperplate or steel engraving. Ivory is softer than the metals, to be sure, and cannot therefore be as closely detailed. Scrimshaw lines must be cut in much more heavily so that they hold the pigment. However, there is a freedom to drawing with broad strokes on ivory in a way which cannot be duplicated on metal, and an entire range of line textures and qualities is possible. Ivory has its own quality.

It is true that composition is limited by the shape of the whale's tooth, but at the same time, the shape provides a great opportunity for the artist to *improvise* a composition. In playing to the sculptural form of the object, the composition gains a kind of life which is not possible on a flat, geometrically bordered surface. This dimensionality of scrimshaw is almost entirely lost in photographic reproductions.

At the time of this writing there is a serious question as to the future availability of the ivories which are the scrimshander's primary material. In 1973 the federal government's *Endangered Species Act* prohibited any further importation of whale's teeth, and it further restricted interstate traffic in teeth already existing in the country, including antique scrimshaw. There was a howl over this, not because anybody objected to the effort to save the endangered whales. That seemed laudable. It appeared counterproductive to limit materials which were already around, however.

Other kinds of ivory are still available at this time, or semi-available. Walrus ivory was restricted, then allowed, then restricted again, due to the machinations of government. Some elephant ivories are restricted, others are allowed. Boar ivory is allowed, Hippopotamus was until quite recently, but now is not. How will all this affect scrimshaw?

On the whole, this artist is optimistic, although seemingly against odds. However, any art form which has survived so many handicaps has a robustness which is very encouraging. After all, the whaling ships are all gone now, but scrimshaw has survived. It has survived without a school of instruction, and survived also being branded a *non-art* by a New Academy which dictates taste as efficiently as the old one did. It has survived the drying up of the materials upon which it relies, and has found others, and— possibly the greatest handicap of all—it has been a fad. Even *that* it has survived.

PLATE 54
A whale ship locked in ice; hunters going out from the ship. *Scrimshaw whale tooth on rosewood spindle stand. 1979*

Notebook sketch. Arctic whaleman with rifle. *Crayon. 1978*

PLATE 55 (detail)
Arctic hunters, steam whalers
and polar scene.
*Scrimshaw walrus tusk on
rosewood base. 1980*

Plate 53 (on page 62) depicts a dockside
scene. At the left, two sailors splice cordage, the
closest one being somewhat distracted by the girl
with the parasol, far right. Also shown are a
stern father and a mother with a leashed dog.
The dog is sniffing a substance on the dock, and
is closely observed by a mother cat, right foreground. A whaling bark is being fitted out. A
sailor rolls a cask, as others set up the jib-boom
rigging.

Plate 54 depicts a whaling ship locked in
arctic ice, drying her sails, as a party of seal hunters and flow-fishermen go out from the ship.

In *plate 55* is another party of arctic hunters, with their ship nearby, the WILLIAM BAYLIES
(a Bath-built whaler converted to steam in 1894).

This is an engraved walrus tusk, one of a set
of seven pieces in all, each a tooth or tusk from
one of the seven major ivory-bearing mammals
(see caption, *plate 64*).

65

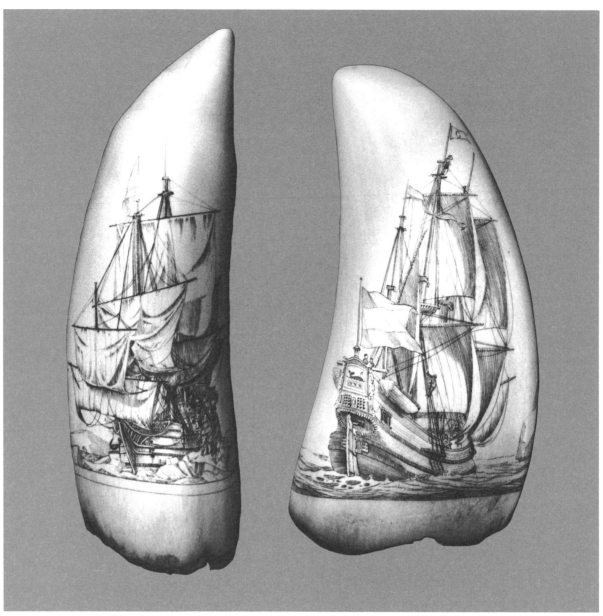

PLATES 56 and 57 (pair)
Dutch whaling fluytes off Greenland.
*Scrimshaw whale teeth on
rosewood spindle stands. 1978, 1979*

Throughout the 1600s the European whaling industry was dominated by the Dutch, who sent hundreds of ships northward into the frigid waters around Spitzbergen and Jan Mayan Land to fish for baleen whales. The vessels they used for whaling were in most respects the same craft that carried cargo in the Dutch merchant service.

Many of these were fluytes, round-sterned (or fluted-stern) vessels, built and rigged for ease of handling.

In 1603 Sir Walter Raleigh complained that a Dutch ship of 100 tons could be worked by a crew of 10 men, while an English ship of equivalent size needed three times that many. How-

PLATES 58 and 59 (pair)
Old Dutch whaling fluyte and
old Dutch whale.
*Scrimshaw whale teeth on
cocobolo wood base. 1980*

ever, all whalers needed larger crews to man their whaleboats.

Dutch whaling fluytes appear in a stern view, *plate 56*, and in a bow view (*plate 57*—a fluyte locked in ice, its crew abandoning ship) and in profile in *plate 59*.

Whereas the three plates listed above show old Dutch whaling vessels, *plate 58* shows an old Dutch whale. This beast will be familiar to any student of whaling lore, for he appears again and again (although with some variations) in engravings from the 1600s, a whiskered, spouting, fanged, gilled whale never photographed in modern times, and therefore thought to be extinct.

Plate 60 illustrates a greatly magnified detail from an engraved whale tooth depicting Yankee whaling barks. In the foreground is a whaleboat under sail, a hard-hatted mate at the helm.

Another whale tooth shows the ship ESSEX of Nantucket "Rammed by an Enraged Sperm Whale & Sunk—Nov 20 1820" as its whaleboats (*plate 62*) look on, helpless.

Plate 61 depicts an American whaling bark in ice, again with hunters sallying forth from the ship. Laundry and sails are both hung out to dry in the still air. On the reverse, *plate 61a*, are hunters with Remington Rolling Block rifles. In

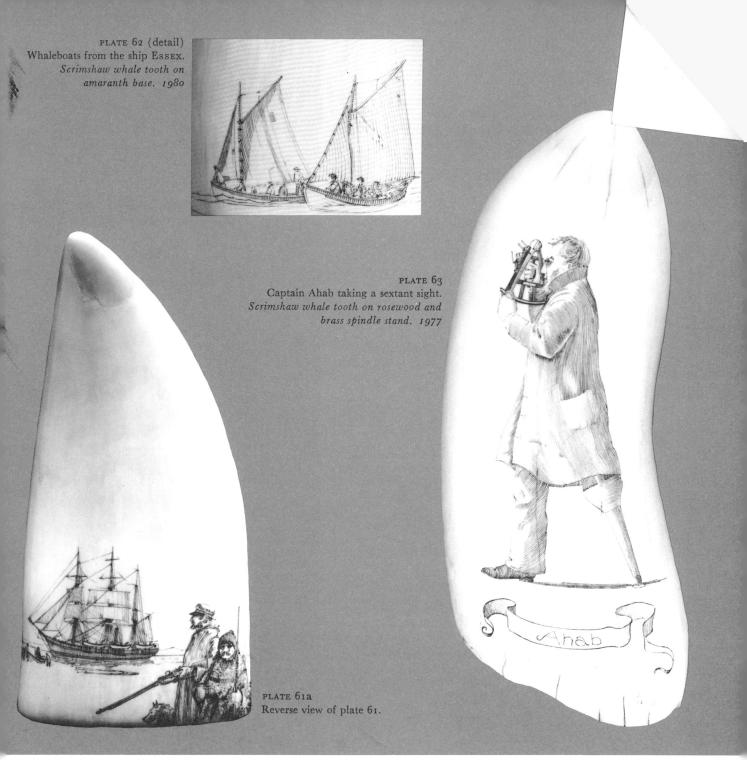

PLATE 62 (detail)
Whaleboats from the ship ESSEX.
*Scrimshaw whale tooth on
amaranth base. 1980*

PLATE 63
Captain Ahab taking a sextant sight.
*Scrimshaw whale tooth on rosewood and
brass spindle stand. 1977*

Ahab

PLATE 61a
Reverse view of plate 61.

the distance is the steam whaler NAVARCH, which was launched in 1892, and was lost in the ice in 1897 near Point Barrow, Alaska. She was abandoned, and 16 of her crew died on their trek across the ice.

In *plate 63* is Captain Ahab, described by Melville, "He looked like a man cut away from the stake, when the fire has overrunningly wasted all the limbs without consuming them, or taking away one particle from their compacted aged robustness. His whole high, broad form seemed made of solid bronze, and shaped in an unalterable mould. . . ." Ahab is scrimshaw'd here taking a sight with his sextant.

69

Plate 64 depicts a scrimshaw work in progress, an elephant tusk in the process of being engraved with a scene depicting a tiger hunt. Sikh beaters accompany elephant-borne hunters. In the background, a sahib peers through binoculars. The elephant in the foreground has caught wind of the tiger. The mahout perceives that something has the elephant's attention, and is pointing, telling the memsahib with the rifle on her knees. It is the moment of the alert.

The elephants and their riders at the left have been engraved in outline. All the other figures and all the areas of tone are rendered in pencil, and are awaiting the knife.

Like the walrus tusk depicted in *plate 55*, this elephant tusk is one of a set of seven scrimshaw pieces, each of which is a tooth or tusk from one of the seven great ivory-bearing mammals, and each of which is engraved with a picture of that animal in his environment. Four of the pieces from this set are indexed here: the elephant (above), the walrus, *plate 55*, and two pieces which are not illustrated: the hippopotamus tusk, item #89, and the killer whale tooth, item #88. The three remaining pieces include the narwhal tusk, the sperm whale tooth, and the boar tusk, all of which are works in progress, scheduled for completion during 1981.

Plate 65 depicts the yacht YANKEE as she appeared around the turn of this century, as a gaff cutter with a jackyard topsail rig. This is one of a pair of whale teeth, the other tooth, *plate 66*, depicts YANKEE as she appeared 75 years later, rerigged as a schooner.

PLATE 64 (detail) A tiger beat with elephants, shikaris, sahibs and tiger.
Scrimshaw elephant tusk (depicted in an unfinished state). 1981

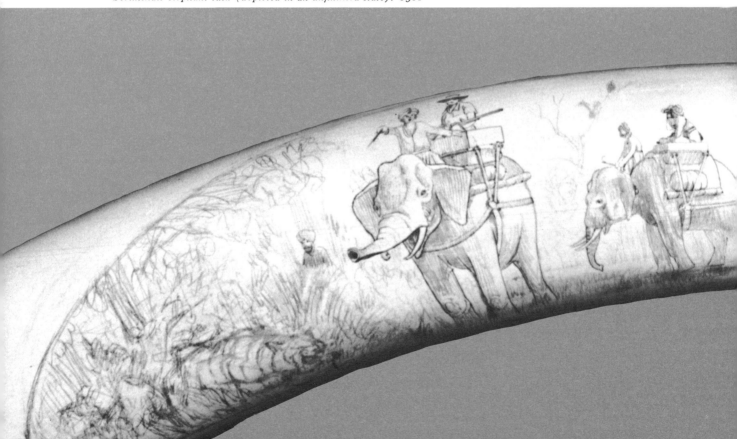

PLATES 65 and 66 (pair)
cht YANKEE as a cutter, c. 1900,
and as a schooner, c. 1975.
*Scrimshaw whale teeth on
common stand.* 1975

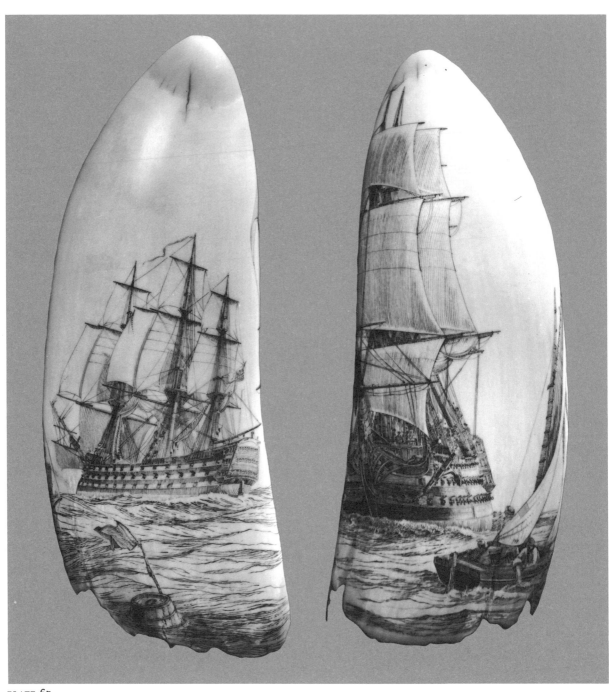

PLATE 67
H.M.S. VICTORY, two views with a
bawley in foreground.
*Scrimshaw whale tooth on rosewood
and brass spindle stand. 1979*

72

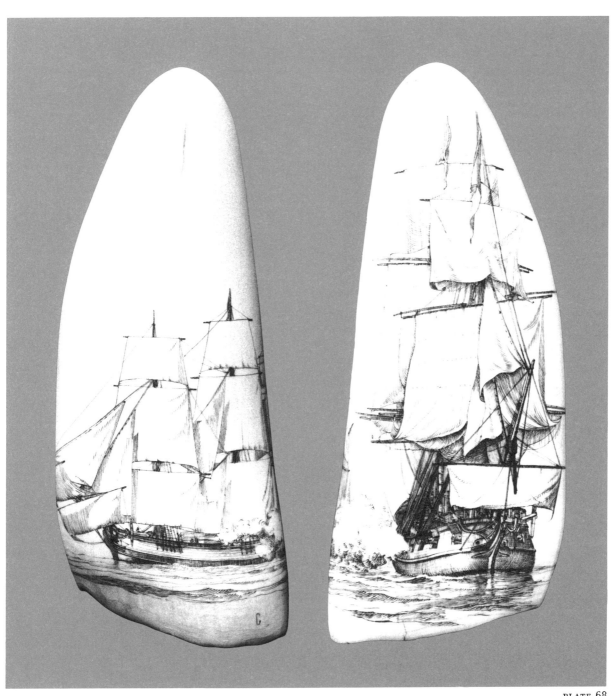

PLATE 68
Continental privateer RATTLESNAKE firing a
signal gun to a merchantman.
*Scrimshaw whale tooth on
yew spindle stand. 1974*

ACKNOWLEDGMENTS

THE GENEROSITY of a great many institutions and individuals has made the MARITIME ARTS BY WM. GILKERSON exhibition and this book possible. The Peabody Museum of Salem and the artist join in expressing thanks and appreciation to all those who have loaned material for display or reproduction: Mr. Robert Anderson, Mr. and Mrs. Dick Callaway, Mr. Michael Edward Carter, Mr. Drayton Cochran, Mr. John Cochran, Dr. Robert Creasy, Mr. Merritt Demarest, Jr., Mr. and Mrs. Giles H. Dunn, Mr. and Mrs. David Eklund, Dr. and Mrs. Burt Fink, Mr. Norman Flayderman, Mr. and Mrs. Albert Ford, Jr., Mr. Peter V. Gammarano, Jr., Mr. and Mrs. Rudy Giesler, Mrs. Kerstin Gilkerson, Mr. Thomas Gillmer, Mr. Thomas L. Harsh, Mr. and Mrs. Tore Helleberg, Mrs. Penelope Hopper, Dr. Barry Lang, Mr. Morgan Levine, Mr. and Mrs. Gordon Lisser, Mr. Norman Mann, Mrs. Sandra Martin, Dr. Bryan J. McSweeney, Jr., the Museum of Fine Arts, Boston, Dr. Norman S. Nadel, The National Maritime Museum of San Francisco, The National Maritime Historical Society, Mr. Walter Roosli, Sea Education Association, Woods Hole, Mass., Mr. and Mrs. Sid Sheehy, Mr. Dean T. Stephens, Mrs. Parker Thomson, The United States Naval Academy Museum, Annapolis, Hon. Paul Vardeman, Dr. John Veirs, Mr. and Mrs. David Bryce Wilson, and Woodenboat Magazine.

Special thanks also go to those whose efforts and talents have contributed to the production of this publication: Mr. John Cochran, Miss Mary Ann Flood, Mrs. Kerstin Gilkerson, Mrs. Miriam Hayden, Mr. Harold Talbott and Mr. Walter Tower.

PLATE 69 (detail)
Women standing on shore, waving to
a departing whaling ship.
*Scrimshaw whale tooth on rosewood
and brass spindle stand. 1979*

Two thousand copies of this book have been printed, of which 1700 are softbound, 261 are hardbound and Arabic numbered, and 39 copies containing an extra plate and an original drawing have been bound for the artist and are numbered I-XXXIX. The type is Baskerville, the paper Monadnock Caress. This book has been designed by the artist and Walter Tower, and has been printed and bound at THE NIMROD PRESS, BOSTON.